Marriage

Sharing Life

"From Grandpa With Love"

Copyright © 2015 Marvin J. Martin

If you find the information beneficial, and you want to pass it on to others, permission is given to reproduce this book, provided the copies are complete, unaltered, and unabridged, including this copyright page, and circulated free of charge.

Unless otherwise noted, Scripture passages are taken from the HOLY BIBLE, NEW INTERNATIONAL VERSION ® Copyright © 1973, 1978, 1984 by International Bible Society. Used by permission of Zondervan Publishing House. All rights reserved

ISBN: 1500376612
ISBN 13: 9781500376611
Library of Congress Control Number: 2014912058
CreateSpace Independent Publishing Platform
North Charleston, South Carolina

The "NIV" and "New International Version" trademarks are registered in the United States Patent and Trademark Office by the International Bible Society. Use of either trademark requires the written permission of the International Bible Society..

A Collection of Later-in-Life Writings

"From Grandpa With Love"

Volume III

*For this reason a man shall leave his father and mother
and be united to his wife,
and the two shall be come one flesh.*
(Genesis 2:24; Ephesians 5:31)

Marriage

This is the third in a series of five *"From Grandpa With Love"* books that consolidate for publication many of the booklets I have been writing over the past thirty-five years to pass on what God was teaching me about life.

We opened the series with an overview of life entitled, *Four Generations: A Journey Through Life.* The next three volumes (*Faith, Marriage,* and *Vocation*) deal with a trio of lifetime decisions we discussed briefly in *Four Generations* as follows:

> As I look back across my life, I see three principal lifetime decisions and three important decision times…The three decisions concern our *Faith,* our *Marriage*, and our *Vocation.* Some have referred to these as our *Master,* our *Mate,* and our *Mission.* The three decision times usually seem to occur toward the end of each generation as we prepare to enter the next season of our lives.

The series concludes with *Passing It On*, discussing the age-old opportunity we have to invest in others what we have experienced and learned during our own journeys.

Once more I say, "*Thank You.*" How grateful I am to the Lord and all those He has used to teach me, help me, and contribute to whatever I have written.

To God Be the Glory!

From Grandpa With Love

Marvin J. Martin
Wichita, Kansas
2015

Contents

Part I	Why Marriage?	1
Part II	Complete—Don't Compete!	15
Part III	Sixty Years of Marriage	83
Part IV	Who Determines the Time to Leave?	105
Part V	Saying Goodbye!	127
Epilogue		151

Part I
Why Marriage?

Then the Lord God made a woman from the rib
he had taken out of the man,
and he brought her to the man.
The man said,
"This is now bone of my bones and flesh of my flesh;
she shall be called 'woman' for she was taken out of man."
For this reason a man will leave
his father and mother and be united to his wife,
and they will become one flesh."
(Genesis 2:22–24. Emphasis added.)

Preface

1992–2008

Dear Family and Friends,

This month Grandma and I will celebrate sixty years of marriage. It has been the most profound, exciting, satisfying human relationship I have ever experienced. Yet, a few days ago I voiced to her once again a statement I have made periodically during all those years: *"You are still somewhat of a mystery to me!"* Probably every married person knows exactly what I mean! And I expect that the mystery will continue until we meet together in Heaven.

This material on "Why Marriage?" was originally written in 1992 both to encourage and to warn of the decline in Biblical marriage that was taking place in American culture. While our own marriage has become even more beautiful to us during these past sixteen years, we have also witnessed marriage in general increasingly attacked, questioned, and abandoned by large segments of society.

The writing is mine, but the concepts and conclusions come from our joint experiences. At ages eighty-one and eighty-three, we probably do not have too many years left. We are more convinced now than ever that faith and traditional marriage (for those He calls) are the bedrock of all God is doing as He prepares His people for eternal life.

Marriage

So, we pass on to you our sense of this great gift that God has given us—with the prayer, hope and plea that you in turn will pass its beauty and mystery on to those who follow you.

From Grandpa With Love,

Why Marriage?

Marriage is a mystery. It has been discussed, analyzed, sometimes idealized, and sometimes disparaged. But, like the union between Christ and His church, it remains a mystery, which we never completely comprehend nor understand. Yet, for all the dimness surrounding it and despite the current attacks upon it, the institution of marriage remains the bedrock of all other human relationships. How we treat one another in this most intimate of relationships designed by God will flow and ripple out into all other relationships and institutions in which we are involved.

It behooves us, therefore, to try and understand first, why God wants marriage to exist; and second, how we can live so that His purpose can be accomplished. Obviously, this is an ideal that will not be fully realized in our fallen world. But to the degree that it happens, we will enjoy marriage, others will be helped and encouraged, and God will be glorified.

There appear to be a least four reasons in Scripture why God created marriage. The first is *Companionship;* the second is *Children;* the third is *Security;* and the fourth is to provide a relationship that is a *Foretaste of Heaven* and attracts the participants and others toward the Kingdom of God.

First: Companionship

Companionship appears to be the most basic and fundamental reason for marriage.

The Bible begins with the account of God's creation of the world. After each of the first items He created, God pronounced that it was "good." However, during the course of His creating, God announced a situation, which He found was *"not* good." After creating one human being, God said:

> *It is not good for the man to be alone.*
> *I will make a helper suitable for him.*
> (Genesis 2:18. Emphasis added.)

So He did!

God reserved the deepest, most intimate companionship between individuals for those who become husbands and wives. It is unique among all relationships. Listen as the Bible describes the creation of *two* individuals out of *one*—who will continue to be *one*, yet *two*!

> *Then the Lord God made a woman from the rib*
> *he had taken out of the man,*
> *and he brought her to the man.*
> *The man said,*
> *"This is now bone of my bones and flesh of my flesh;*
> *she shall be called 'woman' for she was taken out of man."*
> *For this reason a man will leave*
> *his father and mother and be united to his wife,*
> ***and they will become one flesh."***
> (Genesis 2:22–24. Emphasis added.)

How we crave to come together as one, not only physically, but emotionally, mentally and spiritually as well! Yet, how hard it is!

The very closeness we begin to develop can become threatening and cause us to cry out for space and the opportunity to be our own person. Tensions build, which too often break the bonds of marriage. Many echo the frustrated cries of males and females over the centuries: "We can't live with them (our spouses), but we can't live without them!"

Our challenge, of course, is to enjoy the mysterious oneness, which God promised through marriage, while at the same time we retain our uniqueness as the separate individuals God created us to be. This can only happen when we both submit ourselves to Him.

Second: Children

A second reason for marriage is that God's people might "increase in number" by having children. The first blessing and commandment from God was:

> *...male and female he created them.*
> *God blessed them and said to them,*
> **"Be fruitful and increase in number; fill the earth..."**
> (Genesis 1:27b–28a. Emphasis added.)

This command has never been amended nor set aside. While there are Biblical exceptions and provisions for full lives without marriage or children, this general command concerning propagation has been repeatedly affirmed in both the Old and New Testaments. (Genesis 9:1; Jeremiah 29:6; Malachi 2:15a; I Timothy 2:15).

We have now entered into the "Harvest Time" of life that we discussed at length in Volume I *Four Generations*. I can't express to you the excitement we had when our young children were around the house. However, those days were sometimes so busy and there was so much going on that we never realized what we had. Now, it's a more quiet time. We are watching the third generation grow into maturity. What a blessing it is when we get together with our grown children, sometimes individually, sometimes with their spouses, sometimes with their families. How refreshing it is to see the cycle of life go on as youngsters are born and come to maturity as our generation grows older and passes away.

As we attend the weddings of many young friends and the funerals of more and more older friends, we are becoming increasingly aware that these ceremonies flow together to make the continuum of life and that it is all bound together by "family."

Some time ago we attended the funeral of a dear friend that I have known since junior high school. I watched as he went off to war and returned; married and became the father of several children; buried his parents; attended the weddings of his children; and practiced law in the same community for many years.

As his wife, children, grandchildren, extended family and friends gathered together for a memorial service, one of his sons read the following poem, which our friend had written earlier on behalf of the family. It is included here because it captures some of the mysterious, yet continuing and eternal significance of marriage and the family relationship:

Family

I am the family.
I am the husband and wife, the mother and father.
I am their sons and daughters.
I would not exist, one without the other.
I am important.
I give balance, poise and confidence.
I demand discipline, integrity and loyalty.
I live gloriously.
I work, laugh, play, fight, weep, win and fail.
Above all, I love.
Thereby, I survive the ecstasies of success,
And rinse the bitterness of defeat.
I shall exist.
My mother and father die for me.
My sons and daughters live within me.
Thereby, I am honored and perpetuated.
I shall give pride and dignity as long as they are.
I am, I was, I will be.
    Jim Sargent '73

At the conclusion, the son who had read the poem said simply, "Thanks, Dad."

It's at times like this that we realize what a great gift God has given to us through our families. It makes all the struggle and effort worthwhile.

Third: Security

I believe a third major reason for marriage is security, for ourselves and our children through the total commitment of the husband and wife. The world can be a harsh and unyielding environment. To help us survive, God has given us physical and spiritual families. The most basic ingredient of our earthly families, and the foundation upon which the care of young children and older parents is based, is marriage.

The writer of Ecclesiastes (4:9–12) gratefully portrays the security that flows from lives that are committed together:

Two are better than one, because they have a good return for their work; if one falls down, his friend can help him up. But pity the man who falls down and has no one to help him up! Also, if two lie down together, they will keep warm. But how can one keep warm alone? Though one may be overpowered, two can defend themselves. A cord of three strands is not quickly broken.

Transitory relationships, whether in or out of marriage, cannot be completely effective because the parties cannot totally rely on one another for care, comfort, and support. By contrast, the traditional marriage vows carry the following pledge, which operates as a foundation for true commitment and security together for a lifetime:

> To have and to hold,
> From this day forward,
> For better, for worse,
> For richer, for poorer,

> In sickness and in health,
> To love and to cherish,
> According to God's holy ordinance,
> Until death do us part.

Two *are* better than one—especially when the *two* become *one*!

When we have known the wonderful sense of security that comes from such a committed relationship, we know the depth of loss by one recently widowed woman who cried, "Now there is no one who puts me first above everyone else in the world."

Fourth: A Foretaste of Heaven

A fourth reason for marriage is to foster a relationship that is so beautiful when carried out in a Godly fashion that it becomes a foretaste of Heaven and attracts the participants and others toward the Kingdom of God.

In describing the proper relationship between husbands and wives in Ephesians 5:23–32, Paul, five times, compares marriage to Christ and the church—the bride of Christ. Since marriage is compared to the mystery of the union of Christ and the church, it surely must be the most attractive, valuable relationship that can exist between two individuals in this world. When a man and woman commit to marriage "in the Lord" and walk with Him and with one another, they experience the joy of oneness—and at the same time they attract to Christ others who see the benefits of such a union.

Who wouldn't want the warmth and love of a lifetime companion, the joy of children and grandchildren (if God wills), and the peace and security of knowing at least one other person in the world wants nothing but the best for them—and be in a loving relationship compared to the relationship between Christ and the church?

Conclusion

People are increasingly asking, "Why Marriage?" Why not just live together and not be bothered with all the ties and commitments that prevent us from doing what we want, when we want, and with whom we want?

I believe the answer is rather simple—but also quite profound:

**Faith and Family are the bedrock
of all relationships and institutions.
God has ordained them for our own good,
and for the good of everyone else.**

**With this foundation, society flourishes—
without it, mankind breaks apart and we destroy ourselves!**

Thanks be to God for giving us Himself—and Marriage!

Part II
Complete—Don't Compete!

*In the Lord, however, woman is not independent of man,
nor is man independent of woman. For as woman came from man,
so also man is born of woman. But everything comes from God.*
(1 Corinthians 11:11)

A Personal Note

2006

I first started working on the roles of Husband and Wife over forty years ago as our children began moving into marriage age. While my parents seemed to be good role models, it was obvious that I did not know, nor could I pass on to others, what the Bible had to say about marriage. So, just as my wife and I had sought a church home when we began to raise a family, so did I now seek God's wisdom for our marriage and to pass it on to our children.

Today, after fifty-eight years of married life, and observing marriages over several generations, I am more convinced than ever that God does have a plan for our lives, and that He gives us many guidelines and instructions about the roles he calls us to fill, including the roles of Husband and Wife.

The following material has evolved through many forms as the years have gone by. As I studied, lived, and taught about these roles, many people helped me expand and better understand what God had in mind for this deepest of all human relationships. I am deeply indebted to them all.

With gratitude, and thanksgiving to God, to my wife, and to all our children and grandchildren who have displayed such a high view of marriage over the years, I now renew these thoughts, and pass them on once more to all who want to enjoy the "mystery of marriage."

From Grandpa With Love

Complete—Don't Compete!

I. The Goal

This is a message, which is unashamedly in favor of Christian marriage. It is written out of a deep desire to help those of us who God has called into marriage to live out our biblical roles as husbands and wives and thereby build strong lifetime unions for God's glory. Marriage is for our enjoyment and for the well-being of ourselves, our society, and future generations.

This booklet does not have all the answers. In fact, it does not even discuss a whole array of issues that are important to marriage and our life in Christ, such as our relation to other family members, principles of finance, sexual intimacy, and many other vital subjects. But it does try to put together *one* piece of the puzzle, i.e., what really are the biblical roles of husband and wife? How are males and females to "fit" together in the institution we call Christian marriage?

Many of the conclusions that we reach will not be popular in today's culture. However, the real test is whether they properly reflect balanced biblical teachings. As always, each reader has the responsibility to study what is said here and to test it against the Scriptures under the guidance of the Holy Spirit and the counsel of other godly Christians. Only the Scriptures are totally correct and infallible. Hopefully, what is written here that is of God will be heard and applied, and what is not will be silenced and discarded.

Marriage is, of course, a mystery (Ephesians 5:32). It is discussed, analyzed, sometimes idealized, and sometimes disparaged. But, like the union between Christ and His church, it remains a mystery that we never completely comprehend or understand. Yet for all the dimness surrounding it, and despite the current attacks upon it, the institution of marriage remains the bedrock of all other human relationships. How we treat one another in this most intimate of relationships designed by God will flow and ripple out into all other relationships and institutions in which we are engaged.

At a time when lifelong marriage appears to many to be an elusive, almost unreachable goal, it seems imperative that we study carefully God's Word, which ordains this relationship to determine how He tells us that marriage can best succeed. We need this understanding, not only for our own happiness, but for the support and well-being of all future generations.

All marriages, of course, are made up of imperfect people—and two imperfect people can't make a perfect marriage. However, there are many *good* lifetime marriages. Admittedly, they are often battle-scarred veterans who have withstood attacks from within and without, but they, and many of those around them, would conclude that their marriages are good—not perfect, but wholesome and good. This doesn't happen simply by chance. Rather it seems to come from God's grace and the application of His Word. Thus, while we see increasing marriage failures in a part of our society, which is not following Christ and His principles, we also see strong, reasonably successful marriages developing among those who are willing to accept Jesus Christ as their Lord and Savior and to apply His principles to their lives and marriages.

Unfortunately, many marriages in past generations have succeeded because God's principles were applied through the *traditions* of the Christian faith rather than because there was any *personal relationship* with Jesus Christ or a personal understanding and daily application of God's Word. Today, many are abandoning even these traditions! Therefore, unless future generations become aware of their need to have a personal relationship with Jesus *and* to put into practice the lifestyle spelled out in the Bible, many of their lives, including their marriage lives, will likely end in failure from an eternal perspective.

It is for that reason this material has been written. For some, it may discuss principles that are unpopular and difficult to accept. But much of Jesus's teachings are hard. He notes at the end of His great "Sermon on the Mount" that "...small is the gate and narrow the road that leads to life, and only a few find it." Then He makes the following conclusion about our lives and our homes:

> *Therefore everyone who hears these words of*
> *mine and puts them into practice*
> *is like a wise man who built his house*
> *on the rock. The rain came down,*
> *the streams rose, and the winds blew and beat against that house; yet it*
> *did not fall, because it had its foundation on the rock. But everyone who*
> *hears these words of mine and does not put them into practice is like a*
> *foolish man who built his house on sand.*
> *The rain came down, the streams rose,*
> *and the winds blew and beat against that house,*
> *and it fell with a great crash.*
> (Matthew 7:24–27)

Because many are not following biblical principles, our homes are now crashing at an unbelievable rate as one out of two marriages crumble and fall! And alarming numbers are abandoning marriage altogether! Hopefully, followers of Christ will increasingly turn and build their homes on the Rock of Jesus Christ and His Word and thereby produce fruitful, lifetime marriages, rather than continue down the road to destruction by following the traditions and false wisdom of the world that surrounds us.

II. The Roles

...male and female He created them.
(Genesis 1:27b)

Some of the most helpful portions of Scripture that speak specifically to the roles of husband and wife are found in Genesis 1–3; Ephesians 5:22–33; Colossians 3:18–19; 1 Peter 3:1–7; 1 Corinthians 7 and 11:1–16; 1 Timothy 2:9–15; and Proverbs 31:10–31. There are many themes and principles, which need to be applied from these Scriptures and from the totality of God's Word as well as the counsel of other godly Christians in order to produce Godly marriages. However, *one* theme that seems to need to be studied, discussed and applied more specifically than has occurred in the past is that husbands and wives should "*Complete—Not Compete*" with one another in our marriages.

God has designed separate, but related roles for men and women in much of life, including our marriages. We need to accept the roles God has given to us and learn to *complete, not compete*, with our spouses. Honestly helping one another to succeed in our biblical roles as husbands and wives can help build successful, enjoyable, fruitful marriages.

There appear to be four principles for men and women that can strengthen our marriage relationships and help them succeed. These are not legalistic rules, but broad principles that appear as themes throughout the Bible. As one observer put it, "These are God's *ideals*, not His *requirements*, for marriage." There are many more principles, of course, but these four seem especially important. They are hard and costly, but they are worth the effort. They are summarized by four steps for each of the partners:

HUSBAND	WIFE
Lead	Follow
Love	Respect
Provide	Increase
Praise	Glow

In the following pages, we will look at these counterbalancing principles of *Leading and Following, Loving and Respecting, Providing and Increasing,* and *Praising and Glowing* as they help to provide the basis for lifetime, fruitful, enjoyable marriages.

Step 1

Lead and Follow

A. Lead

Now I want you to realize that the head of every man is Christ, and the head of the woman is man, and the head of Christ is God.
(1 Corinthians 11:3)

God in His sovereignty has assigned roles, including strengths and limitations, to all His people. While we are equally *valuable* in His sight, our *functions* vary. He assigns our locations and our times (Acts 17:26). He makes the blind and the deaf (Exodus 4:11). He knows us before we are born (Psalm 139:13–16). He makes us male and female (Genesis 1:27). He not only assigns our mental and physical characteristics and abilities, but also distributes His spiritual gifts upon us as He wills (1 Corinthians 12:11).

Leadership in the Bible
Despite the tremendous societal pressure against this position today, the Bible reveals that the role of leadership during Bible times was usually, although not always, men's responsibility. For example:

1. God made man first, then woman, and decreed that man would "*rule over*" his wife. (Genesis 2:7, 18–23, 3:16)
2. It was Eve who was deceived and first ate the forbidden fruit. However, because Adam *followed* his wife rather

than exercising the responsibility of leadership he had been given by God, it was *Adam*, not Eve, who has been credited through history as the person responsible for man's fall. (Genesis 3; Romans 5:12–21)
3. Virtually all Old Testament Jewish leaders (in their families, tribes, nation, temple, and synagogues) were men.
4. All Books of the Bible—both the Old and New Testament—appear to have been written by men.
5. In the New Testament, all the twelve Apostles chosen by Jesus were men.
6. The responsibilities of New Testament "elders" were directed to men (1Timothy 3:1–7) who were also to manage their own families well. (v. 4–5) (See also Titus 1:6–9)
7. The role of the wife as a "helper" rather than "head" of the family is a consistent theme throughout both the Old and New Testaments. (Genesis 2:18; 1 Corinthians 11:3, 14:33–35; 1 Timothy 2:11–15; Ephesians 5:22–24; Colossians 3:18; 1 Peter 3:1)

While there are occasional references to Godly leaders, (such as Deborah, the Judge), and to prophetic gifts used by a few women (such as Miriam, the sister of Moses, in the Old Testament [Exodus 15:20] and Phillip's daughters in the New Testament [Acts 21:9]), the great preponderance of evidence seems to make it clear that men carried most of the burden of leadership in both Old and New Testament times.

Defining Leadership
In order to understand the role of the husband as the "leader" of the family, let's first define this term. The world often

equates leadership with power, prestige, and privilege. The Bible says leadership requires service. Jesus compared these two views this way:

> *Jesus called them together and said,*
> *"You know that the rulers of the Gentiles lord it over them,*
> *and their high officials exercise authority over them.*
> *Not so with you. Instead, whoever wants to become*
> *great among you must be your servant,*
> *and whoever wants to be first must be your slave—*
> *just as the Son of Man*
> *did not come to be served, but to serve,*
> *and to give his life as a ransom for many."*
> (Matthew 20:25–28)

Leadership is not the same as command. Command is the legal authority that forces a subordinate to obey. The Centurion understood this principle as he said:

> *For I myself am a man under authority,*
> *with soldiers under me.*
> *I tell this one, "Go," and he goes;*
> *and that one, "Come," and he comes.*
> *I say to my servant, "Do this," and he does it.*
> (Luke 7:8)

Military officers can command their subordinates, parents can command their children, and supervisors can even command their employees, as long as the law (including the law of the institution) and public policy are not violated. Command, therefore, depends upon *authority*. Those under such authority are *required* to obey.

Servant Leadership
By contrast, biblical leadership depends upon an individual being so *attractive* that others *want* to follow. Leaders neither drive nor abandon their subordinates: they *serve* them.

As we analyze the question of leadership, it causes us to ask, "Who was the greatest leader who ever lived?" The answer, of course, is Jesus Christ. Over one billion people follow Jesus Christ today. Not because they are *required* to do so, but because they *desire* to do so!

What is the quality that causes so many to submit and to follow Him? At least part of the answer is found in John 13. It was the night before Jesus was betrayed. John recounts how Jesus began to wash His disciples' feet. When He came to Peter, this Apostle responded as we probably would if our "leader" began to serve us in this menial fashion, and he told Jesus, "…you shall never wash my feet." Jesus said unless He did, Peter couldn't have any part of Him, so Peter acquiesced. When Jesus had completed His servant's task, He told His Apostles that they called Him "Teacher" and "Lord," and so He was, but that He had done this service as an example and they should do likewise.

The message is clear: Those who lead must serve.

Be Strong Enough to Lead
It requires strength, courage, and self-sacrifice to lead. But it will set the tone for everything else that occurs in our marital relationships. Unless the husband is strong enough to lead, the wife cannot follow. The wife intuitively knows her husband must be strong enough to lead, so she may test him to determine whether

she is safe in her role as "helper" or whether she needs to take charge in order to protect herself and her children. As one husband put it, "Your wife will fight you for the leadership of your marriage, but be terribly disappointed if she wins."

Husbands must lead.

How Does a Real Leader "Lead?"
Makes time for people—We are attracted to those people who have time for us. One individual, speaking about the person who had the greatest impact upon his life, said, "He always had time for me." If husbands truly want to lead their wives, they must make time for them.

Finds ways to serve—Leaders serve those who follow them in order that the followers may succeed in the work they are called to do. The paradox is that, while the wife is to be a "helper" to the husband, she often cannot succeed in this unless he first serves her. We will discuss at length below the ways in which husbands provide for and protect their wives in order that wives can succeed in the work they are called to do

Stays in front and in motion—We cannot lead from behind or sitting down. It requires that we be in front and that we be in motion. This is called the "point" position in the military. It is the person who often gets shot at first. It is the person who leads the way in difficult situations rather than allowing their subordinates to lead. Jesus repeatedly said, "Follow me," as he demonstrated the way for us. Husbands have this same obligation and opportunity with their wives and family.

Cares about those who follow—There are all kinds of leaders: fiery and quiet, athletic and intellectual, bombastic and deliberate, but they all have one thing in common if they are successful leaders—they care about their followers. While followers want to know that their leaders love Jesus, they also want to know that they care about their followers. As one wife said, "I don't want you to do it just for Jesus, I want you to do it for me." All followers need the assurance that they are deeply loved.

Both Moses and Paul exhibited an almost unbelievable amount of love for their followers: to the point that they were apparently willing to lose their own eternal salvation in their great desire for their followers to receive the salvation and love of God. For example, when the Israelites sinned, Moses said to God:

> *But now, please forgive their sin—but if not,*
> *Then blot me out of the book you have written.*
> (Exodus 32:32)

And Paul, speaking about the Jews who would not accept Christ said:

> *For I could wish that I myself were cursed*
> *and cut off from Christ for the sake of my brothers,*
> *those of my own race...*
> (Romans 9:3)

Leaders who exhibit this kind of care toward their followers can expect their followers to follow them.

Learn to Follow

This brings us to an interesting point. As the roles of husbands and wives and the four elements of *Lead, Love, Provide,* and *Praise* and their counterparts of *Follow, Respect, Increase,* and *Glow* were being discussed by a group, one of the participants said, "Actually, the husband must be in the same position to Christ as the wife is to the husband." What an astute observation!

When we superimpose this concept of the husband's submission to Christ on our diagram, it causes it to look like this:

CHRIST	**HUSBAND**
Lead	Follow
Love	Respect
Provide	Increase
Praise	Glow

HUSBAND	**WIFE**
Lead	Follow
Love	Respect
Provide	Increase
Praise	Glow

Unless the husband is willing to demonstrate this submission to his leader, Christ, he creates rebellion among those who should follow him. One wife made this clear to her husband as she inquired, "Do you know when I became willing to follow you?"

"When?" he asked.

"When I saw you follow Jesus!" she responded.

Thus, when we look at each element of the wife's role, it is clear that husbands are to carry out this subordinate role to Christ before they exercise the role of leader in their families. For example:

Follow Jesus said:

> *Then he said to them all: "If anyone would*
> *come after me, he must deny himself*
> *and take up his cross daily and follow me."*
> (Luke 9:23)

Respect Scriptures are replete with the theme of fearing (respecting) God. For example:

> *Now all has been heard; here is the conclusion of the matter:*
> *Fear God and keep his commandments,*
> *for this is the whole duty of man.*
> (Ecclesiastes 12:13)

Increase God, at the very beginning of the world, gave mankind the responsibility to increase and to subdue what He had handed to them.

> *God blessed them and said to them,*
> *"Be fruitful and increase in number,*
> *fill the earth and subdue it.*
> *Rule over the fish of the sea and the birds of the air*
> *and over every living creature that moves on the ground."*
> (Genesis 1:28; see also Genesis 9:7)

Glow All of us would ultimately like to glow and reflect our Maker. We would be like Moses when he came down from God's presence with his face so radiant that he veiled it:

> *When Moses finished speaking to them,*
> *he put a veil over his face.*
> *But whenever he entered the Lord's presence to speak with him,*
> *he removed the veil until he came out.*
> *And when he came out and told the Israelites*
> *what he had been commanded,*
> *they saw that his face was radiant.*
> *Then Moses would put the veil back over his face*
> *until he went in to speak with the Lord.*
> (Exodus 34:33–35)

Or Stephen, whose face shown like an angel as he proclaimed Jesus immediately before he was stoned to death (Acts 6:15).

Husbands, therefore, need to follow Christ, then be a model of His humble, servant leadership to their wives. Both husbands and wives can then exercise such servant leadership to their children.

B. Follow

> *In the Lord, however, woman is not independent of man,*
> *nor is man independent of woman.*
> (1 Corinthians 11:11)

Submission in the Bible

This brings us to the question of wives following and submitting to the leadership of husbands. There is no question that this is a great theme of the Bible. For example:

> *To the woman he said, "I will greatly increase your pains*
> *in childbearing; with pain you will give birth to children.*
> *Your desire will be for your husband, and he will rule over you."*
> (Genesis 3:16)

> *Wives, submit to your husbands as to the Lord.*
> *For the husband is the head of the wife*
> *as Christ is the head of the church,*
> *his body, of which he is the Savior.*
> (Ephesians 5:22–23)

> *Wives, submit to your husbands, as is fitting in the Lord.*
> (Colossians 3:18)

> *A woman should learn in quietness and full submission.*
> *I do not permit a woman to teach or to have authority over a man;*
> *she must be silent.*
> (1Timothy 2:11–12)

> *Wives, in the same way be submissive to your husbands*
> *so that, if any of them do not believe the word,*
> *they may be won over without words*
> *by the behavior of their wives…*

> *For this is the way the holy women of the past*
> *who put their hope in God*
> *used to make themselves beautiful.*
> *They were submissive to their own husbands...*
> (1 Peter 3:1,5)

> *Now I want you to realize that the head of every man is Christ,*
> *and the head of the woman is man, and the head of Christ is God.*
> (1 Corinthians 11:3)

> *Then they can train the younger women*
> *to love their husbands and children,*
> *to be self-controlled and pure, to be busy at home,*
> *to be kind and to be subject*
> *to their husbands, so that no one will malign the word of God.*
> (Titus 2:4–5)

These are not isolated, out-of-context statements, but a consistent theme.

But is it a proper position for wives today? Is it demeaning to be a follower? To analyze this issue, let's look at several questions.

First, are followers less valuable?

Jesus Himself pointed the way on this issue. He demonstrated the difference between *function* and *value*. *Functionally*, Jesus subordinated himself to God the Father to carry out His role on earth (1 Corinthians 11:3). But this subordination did not lower His *value*, as shown by the Scripture that tells us that Jesus contains all of God (Colossians 1:19).

Followers are not less valuable than leaders.

Second, is it "unfair" for wives to have the role of "follower?"
God assigns as He wills. He emphasized men's inability to have children when He asked Jeremiah the rhetorical question:

> *Ask and see: Can a man bear children?*
> (Jeremiah 30:6)

By contrast, Jesus, in speaking of a woman's role in bearing children, said:

> *A woman giving birth to a child has pain because her time has come;*
> *but when her baby is born she forgets the anguish because of her joy*
> *that a child is born into the world.*
> (John 16:21)

A man will never feel a child in his womb nor know the deep pain followed by the marvelous joy of birth of a new life into the world. Never will he hold a child to nurse at his breast as his nourishment flows into and gives life to his child. Is God unfair to men (or to women who are unable to bear children)? No! No matter how much we protest and complain, we cannot, nor should we desire to, change what God has made.

By the same rationale, God is not unfair to the wife when He assigns to her husband rather than to her the pain and joy of leadership while ordinarily giving her the pain and joy of bearing children (1 Timothy 2:15). Neither a husband nor a wife is less valuable than the other. They are only carrying out their different functions. They are not meant to *compete* with one another by both leading or by both giving birth to children, but rather to *complete* one another by carrying out their separate roles.

Third, is it beneficial for wives to follow?
Husbands and wives are different in many ways. Yet, they are joined. 1 Peter 3:7 (RSV) says they are "joint heirs of the grace of life." Like joint owners in property holdings, a husband and wife are two and yet one.

Husbands and wives have so much to give and to receive from one another. But part of what God has for a husband he must receive through his wife. Part of what He has for her will of necessity flow through her husband. How tragic if either of them attempts to compete with the other's position, rather than functioning in their own position and blessing them both.

Take, for example, the way we look at life. In general, husbands seem to look outward, to see into the distance, like a telescope pointing toward infinity. By contrast, the wife traditionally looks inward as if looking through a microscope for the details. While he is usually concerned with long-term goals, she is often making sure the family is well clothed and cared for today.

But, we ask, which way is infinity farther—outward through the telescope or inward through the microscope? Both are infinite. And, which is more important—to see infinity outwardly, or inwardly? Both are equally valuable. But what a tragedy if husbands and wives *compete* by both trying to view life only through two telescopes pointed outward or through two microscopes pointed inward. *If they compete, they do not complete, and both are poorer.* Ultimately, their dissatisfaction can lead them further apart. How wonderful if they *complete* one another by each looking through their respective lenses and sharing what they learn.

Finally, what about interdependence?
The real answer, of course, is not *independence* of husbands, nor *dependence* of wives, but *interdependence* of husbands and wives. First Corinthians 11:11–12 says:

> *In the Lord, however, woman is not independent of man, nor is man independent of woman. For as woman came from man, so also man is born of woman. But everything comes from God.*

How ironic! The first woman came from man. Every other man has come from a woman. God has not made us independent, nor dependent. Instead, he has made husbands and wives *interdependent*.

First Peter 3:1 of the Living Bible encourages wives to "fit in with" their husband's plans. As a young couple approached an onlooker one day, he realized that they actually fit together, physically. The man had broad shoulders and narrow hips; the wife was just the opposite. "Why?" the observer asked himself. Then it became clear to him. A function of the wife is to "carry" men from gestation through birth and infancy. The responsibility of husbands is to "carry" women when they are grown, especially when they are large and limited due to carrying (and caring for) children.

Oneness

God does not want competition between husbands and wives. He states in both the Old and New Testaments that He wants oneness.

> *For this reason a man will leave his father and mother*
> *and be united to his wife, and they will become one flesh.*
> (Genesis 2:24; Ephesians 5:31)

He wants us to have the fullness known in no other way than can happen in marriage. It is so sacred and wonderful that only the analogy of Christ Himself and His own bride can show its riches and fullness (Ephesians 5:22–32).

Step 2

Love and Respect

A. Love

*However, each of you also must love his wife
as he loves himself...*
(Ephesians 5:33a)

The key to the Christian life is love. When we submit ourselves to another, or, as it has been said, "put ourselves under the protection of another," such action calls forth in them a desire to love and care for us. True, it can also give them the opportunity to use and abuse us. But those who are controlled by the spirit of God will see the opportunity and responsibility to love and care for their followers—whether it be a wife and children in the family, employees in business, members in the church, or citizens in government. Leaders in each of these institutions will have to account to God for their use of this responsibility and power (e.g., Hebrews 13:17; Colossians 4:1).

Defining Biblical Love
There are many discussions about "love" in both the Old and the New Testaments. But what is biblical "love" and how does a husband practice it with his wife? In response to a question, Jesus summarized the Great Commandment of the *Old* Testament as follows:

*Jesus replied: "'Love the Lord your God with all your heart
and with all your soul and with all your mind.'
This is the first and greatest commandment.*

> *And the second is like it: 'Love your neighbor as yourself'.*
> *All the Law and the Prophets hang on these two commandments."*
> (Matthew 22:37–39. Emphasis added.)

But when He Himself was preparing to leave His disciples, He gave them a *new* Commandment, which characterized the boundless, sacrificial love of Christ.

> *A new command I give you: Love one another.*
> *As I have loved you, so you must love one another.*
> *By this all men will know that you are my disciples,*
> *if you love one another.*
> (John 13:34–35. Emphasis added.)

The definition of this new boundless love that we are to emulate is found in 1 John 3:16:

> *This is how we know what love is:*
> *Jesus Christ **laid down his life** for us.*
> *And we ought to **lay down our lives** for our brothers.*
> (Emphasis added.)

And it is this same boundless love that Paul uses to describe a husband's responsibility to his wife:

> *Husbands, love your wives,*
> ***just as Christ loved the church and gave himself up for her***
> *to make her holy, cleansing her by the washing with water*
> *through the word, and to present her to himself*
> *as a radiant church, without stain or wrinkle or any other blemish,*

> *but holy and blameless.*
> *In this same way, husbands ought to love their wives*
> *as their own bodies.*
> *He who loves his wife loves himself.*
> (Ephesians 5:25–28. Emphasis added.)

The husband, as the leader of the family, is to lead in demonstrating this kind of love. It is not that he is not to respect his wife. To the contrary, as Peter says in his first letter:

> *Husbands, in the same way be considerate as you live*
> *with your wives, and treat them with respect as the weaker partner*
> *and as heirs with you of the gracious gift of life,*
> *so that nothing will hinder your prayers.*
> (1 Peter 3:7)

But this respect for a wife is not listed first. Instead, it seems to be the result of recognizing and accepting the responsibility to love and care for this partner who, because of God's design, has been called to function as the "weaker" vessel who subordinates herself and is willing to make herself vulnerable by childbirth (if that is God's plan for her)—unable to defend herself because of the awkward disability that carrying, bearing, and caring for children will bring.

How Do Husbands Give Themselves Up for Their Wives?

The question is often asked, "How does a husband 'give himself up' for his wife?" Much of this comes by *Providing* for and *Praising* his wife, as we will discuss below. But there are also some other practical ways. For example:

Be There!

Breadwinners can become so caught up in their role as achievers in the work world that they abandon the role of loving their families. A young woman was once asked, "How do you know if someone loves you?" She quickly responded, "If they want to be with you."

The answer is sound. One of the ways we demonstrate our love for anyone, including God, is to spend time with them.

Spending time physically is not enough. As one wife said, "I would rather he were not here than to be here when he is not here." In other words, one of the ways a husband gives himself up for his wife is when he gives her his *whole* self when they are together. When he listens to his wife, not out of duty, but out of interest. When he is interested in what his wife is interested in. When he weeps as his wife weeps and rejoices as she rejoices. In all these things, a husband demonstrates that he is laying down his life for his wife.

Be a Lover

1 Corinthians 13 is the great New Testament chapter on "love." Verses four to seven provide a broad checklist for husbands to use as they lead in demonstrating love for their wives. This "love list," like the activities of the "Godly woman" spelled out in Proverbs 31, is overwhelming and impossible for any one person to perform. However, it's not impossible for God to perform through us. God is love. If we concentrate on giving ourselves up and allowing Him to live and act through us, He can bring this quality of love into our marriage. By *His grace*, then, a husband needs to try:

To be patient with his wife (and others). It is easy to be impatient, especially with a subordinate. When waiting for dinner at home or leaving for an evening out, is the husband disgusted because of delays, or does he thank God for the privilege of learning the godly quality of patience?

To be kind to his wife (and others). The quality of kindness relates to feelings. By nature, women often seem to be more sensitive than men. A husband's actions (and inactions), his choice of words, and his tone of voice, often tell her sensitive ears and eyes whether he is being kind or callous.

Not to envy his wife (or others). Husbands need to release their wives to be the persons God called them to be. Writings in the New Testament do not appear to give the husband the right to command his wife to submit and follow his directions. Instead, the burden seems to be on the wife to submit *voluntarily* in obedience to God's command.

Not to boast to his wife (or others). It is easy to become a bore. All it takes is constantly telling others about our abilities and successes. When we truly love others, we try to give ourselves up and concentrate on helping them to succeed.

Not to exhibit pride to his wife (or others). Pride may be a man's greatest enemy. Husbands are anointed with leadership, not to be called great, but to serve those who follow. If husbands forget this, they may treat their wives as less valuable. They also may unconsciously pressure them to act in a way that will elevate the husband's position in the eyes of the world. Paul says it this way:

> *Do nothing out of selfish ambition or vain conceit,*
> *but in humility consider others better than yourselves.*
> *Each of you should look not only to your own interests,*
> *but also to the interests of others.*
> (Philippians 2:3–4)

Not to be rude to his wife (or to others). Leadership brings the opportunity to feel much more important than we are. What a husband does in the world may sometimes seem more important to him than the home-centered activities of his wife. If that happens, he can push his wife into a less valuable role. Then it can become a way of life as he feels the importance of his role gives him license to be rude to others, including his wife.

Not to be self-seeking from his wife (or others). Being in the lead can tempt us to seek the best for ourselves. What an ungodly life and improper example and model is displayed when a position of leadership is used to enhance the leader's own comfort, security, pleasure, or position!

Not to be easily angered by his wife (or others). It is easy to display anger against or in the presence of those who are weaker and won't retaliate. By contrast, we exercise great self-discipline, we "count to ten," and we control our anger in the presence of those who are stronger or more powerful. How sad the increasing tendency of some men to verbally and physically abuse women and children rather than to love and care for them and to serve them so they can succeed in life.

Not to keep a record of wrongs with his wife (or others). Twice in Hebrews, the Old Testament is quoted to show that God actually *forgets our sins* (Hebrews 8:12 and 10:17). If God does this for sinful husbands, how can they do less for their wives? Saying we will "forgive" but we will "never forget" is a contradiction in terms. Love cannot be complete until we "forget" and no longer discuss nor dwell on past wrongs. As the Lord's Prayer states, "Forgive us as we forgive others."

Not to rejoice in evil but in the truth of his wife (or others). Sometimes we use other's mistakes as an excuse or justification for our own bad thoughts, words, or conduct. We begin to think negatively and dwell on the percentage of each other person that is imperfect—rather than praising the good and helping them move closer to the image of Christ. When a husband sees his wife as a creature who God is bringing to perfection, he is motivated to do all he can to help her succeed, just as he wants her to help him be successful in order that they may mutually enjoy one another and that God may be glorified through their marriage.

To protect his wife (and others). If a wife is truly a husband's jewel and his most important person, he will go to all possible lengths to protect her and others who are within his area of responsibility.

To trust his wife (and others). Most of us react the way we are treated. If we mistrust, we build suspicion and doubt in the other person. If we trust, it can usually become a self-fulfilling prophecy that produces the best that was in the other person.

To hope for his wife (and others). As the leader in marriage, the husband can often set its tone. If he looks confidently toward the future, he builds confidence and hope in his wife. By contrast, if a husband despairs and dwells in doubt and gloom, he can expect his wife to react accordingly.

To persevere with his wife (and others). One of the great hallmarks of lifetime marriages is perseverance. As one person put it, "We are still married because we decided to be." Or, as another one stated, "Divorce was never an option." There are times in every marriage when separation and divorce could be sought under our current lax divorce laws. But we do well not only to persevere, but never even to contemplate divorce, since such thoughts have a way of leading to action. If divorce is not an option, it makes marriage commitment much more a matter of fact, rather than a burden.

Only a few things are eternal and totally reliable. One of these is love. First Corinthians 13:8 in the New International Version says, "Love never fails." In the Revised Standard Version, it is translated, "Love never ends." Both are right. How wonderful to know that the love of God that flows from Him back and forth through a husband and wife is something that is totally reliable and will last forever. How wonderful to know that this love can go through eternity with both a husband and wife, and they can go through eternity through the grace and love of God. How wonderful that He gives us a foretaste of heaven now through giving and receiving love, beginning with the love of a husband for his wife that He compares to Christ and the church.

B. Respect

...and the wife must respect her husband.
Ephesians 5:33b

Motivated by Love
Looking forward, we are motivated by either hope of gain or fear of loss. In the spiritual realm, that means heaven or hell. Looking backward, we are motivated by gratitude or revenge. Of all these, the most mature motivation seems to be gratitude for what we have already received. Thus, we do not work for Christ in order to receive our future salvation, instead we submit our life to Him to use us as He will out of gratitude for the great sacrifice He has already performed for us and all the rest of mankind.

The same would appear to be true of motivation between husband and wife. While we are tempted to act right in order to receive a future reward from our spouse, the most mature motivation is to act out of gratitude for the past. Thus, a Godly wife who sees her husband love and give himself up for her as Christ did for the church is deeply stirred with gratitude. She is a natural reactor. She usually responds as she is treated. If she is driven or abandoned, she can be expected to act with resistance or independence; but if she is loved, as Christ loved the church, it will ordinarily bring forth in her an overwhelming sense of gratitude and respect. She will usually come to respect and love her husband, not to compete or to fight with him, because he first loved her.

It is interesting that in discussing the husband-wife relationship in Ephesians 5, 1 Timothy 2, and 1 Peter 3, nowhere does it command the wife to love their husband. A wife's desire to love her husband will usually flow automatically from receiving love from him. In speaking of God's love, the Apostle John said, "We love because He first loved us" (I John 4:19). The same is surely true of love between husband and wife. As the leader, the husband is commanded to love his wife. She in turn is to respect and ultimately to love him in return. In addition, Paul explained to Titus that wives are to be *trained* by older women to love their husbands (Titus 2:4), probably because true Christian love may take years to develop and mature.

Many wives, of course, love their husbands long before the husband loves them. Yet that doesn't appear to be God's *best* plan for a strong marriage. Instead, men are commanded to *lead* in loving and giving themselves up for their wives and families. Their failure to do so has been one of the great complaints and rationale for women needing to step into the male role, as they are now increasingly doing in single-parent families and in business, church, and government. Because men have sometimes abused their wives and children or abdicated from their responsibility to lead and to love those who follow them, many women have had no choice but to accept the responsibilities God designated for men as the head of the household. But this is second best!

Man's Great Yearning
Men seem to need respect from their wives even before they need love. Men can be encouraged by the respect, or greatly damaged by the lack of respect, given to them—especially by their wives. Husbands need to know that their wife, as their closest confidante and most important critic, respects what they are doing in life. Women receive a sense of fulfillment (and great respect in earlier generations) from having children. But men have no children to come from their bodies. While men may deeply love and care for their children, they can never have the same sense of physical oneness with them as mothers who spend nine months in total physical union with the child, and then bring forth into the world an infant who they cuddle and feed, often from their own bodies.

For this reason, men desperately need their wives' respect about the work that they are doing, just as she needs encouragement in the role of a wife and mother that God has given to her. One discouraged husband almost abandoned his God-given gift of teaching God's Word as he cried out, "I think I'll quit teaching. My wife seems embarrassed or on edge about everything I say in class." Another husband seemed almost to "wilt" as his wife publicly criticized his incorrect language in a small crowd at a party when she said, "Oh, he always talks like that. He never uses correct English."

A too-common complaint among men seems to be: "I can't ever please her."

Respect Toward the Office
For these reasons, a wife should cultivate the habit of respecting her husband, not because of his actions, but because of his

office. He, like the judge in the courtroom, or the ruler of a church body, deserves respect simply because he is the husband, appointed by God to lead his family. Treating him with respect enhances and affirms his office and his ability to carry out his role. Disrespect can cause him to lose his self-esteem and never become the husband he could have been. If this happens, everyone loses: the husband, the wife, their children, their extended family, friends, and society as a whole.

Criticism and Control
We should be very careful about criticizing others (Matthew 7:1–5). This is especially true for wives, who need to help meet their husbands' need for respect.

Neither should wives attempt to control their husband's future. Some women seem to see (like Michelangelo) a statue of David in the block of granite who is called their husband. But a wife cannot force this figure into existence. Instead, she can only respect and patiently encourage and help him as he emerges and blossoms through God's grace to be the husband God had designed.

This doesn't mean that she is not to reprove him. Few people love us enough to tell us for our own benefit where we err. Husbands desperately need this kind of honest reproof, especially from our own wives who know us best. The key seems to be whether or not the statement is made for retaliation or for the success of the hearer. And the tone and tenor of the reproof is often the way the true attitude is revealed.

Be Careful about the Counsel of Other Men

Men may find it difficult to compete with other men for their wives' respect. Negatively comparing a husband to another man can be destructive. In addition, wives receiving counsel from other men may cause problems. Perhaps that's why St. Paul instructed Titus to *teach* the *older* women who in turn could *train* the *younger* women how to love their husbands (Titus 2:3–5). Such training is an important ministry for older women, that badly needs to be accepted and taught, rather than placing the full burden of such training on already overworked pastors and other professional counselors.

Be Wives and Not Mothers to Husbands

Some women, unfortunately, attempt to extend their "mother instinct" to the relationship with their husbands, and sometimes an immature husband will feel comfort in this child role. It has been said, "A woman should be careful of becoming attached to a man looking for a mother." It may provide an outlet for certain emotions, but it probably won't be the basis for a strong marriage.

Step 3

Provide and Increase

A. Provide

*After all, no one ever hated his own body,
but he feeds and cares for it, just as Christ does the church.*
(Ephesians 5:29)

Motivating Husbands to Provide
It is difficult for women to understand or comprehend how much a man wants to provide for a wife who follows and respects him. It arouses in him all the manliness he possesses. He becomes far greater than he felt he could become because he realizes she is dependent on him to care for her. There are many needs a husband can provide that will strengthen a marriage.

Economic Needs
A wife who was trying to implement biblical teaching in her life told this story:

> "Shortly after my husband and I became Christians, I knew that I needed a particular item, as my old one was wearing out. In the past, I had tried to convince my husband to get me the very best possible, but in our economic condition, it was always modest. This time, I decided simply to rely on him to provide for me as the Scriptures had commanded. When he asked me what I wanted, I told him I was just looking for him to provide

as he thought best. To my surprise, he brought home a beautiful **new** gift, which was much more than I would have requested."

She had learned a valuable lesson. A Godly husband *wants* to provide the *very best he can* for a Godly wife who respects and follows him. It gives both of them pleasure when this happens.

Unfortunately, as women pursue careers outside the home, they become more and more economically independent, and there is less reason for the man to feel a responsibility to provide for her. In fact, in the short term, her working relieves his economic burden, and he can begin not only to condone but to encourage it. As he does so, they receive short-term economic help, but they may sow the seeds for later difficulties. It is not that Godly wives are not to have wealth, nor to be income-producers. Jesus himself was supported by women from their "own means" (Luke 8:1–3). Lydia in the New Testament (Acts 16:14), as well as the "proverbial Godly woman" in Proverbs 31 that we will discuss later, both make it clear that Godly women often have engaged in producing income. It seems, however, the question is whether or not she *majors* in being a wife (and usually a mother) while carrying on some economic activity as a *minor* part of her responsibility *in conjunction with the home, not in competition to it.*

Occupation. A husband must, of course, be prepared to provide for a wife when they become married. When a father answers the questions, "Who gives this woman to be married to this man?" it signifies the passing of responsibility to the new husband for the provision and protection of his new bride.

In this modern world, it means the husband must be trained so that he is ready, willing, and able to provide for the economic needs of himself, his wife, and their family. While this may mean some initial sacrifice, it will pay large dividends in maintaining a lifetime marriage relationship. As Proverbs says:

> *Finish your outdoor work and get your fields ready;*
> *after that, build your house.*
> (Proverbs 24:27)

Home. If a wife is to center her career at home, the husband needs to provide a dwelling and furnishings as tools for her work. Just as he needs tools for his vocation, so does she for hers. Because of current market values, many can often begin, at least, by renting rather than buying—and not be saddled with the problems of home ownershipsale in our mobile society.

Debt. There are many areas in which economists disagree. But one area of increasing agreement among Christian financial advisors is the undesirability of debt. In our government, our businesses, and our personal lives, we have placed enormous burdens on ourselves through massive debt. Proverbs 22:7 says:

> *The rich rule over the poor,*
> *and the borrower is servant to the lender.*

We have moved from being the largest creditor nation to the largest debtor nation in the world in just a few short years. Bankruptcy courts are full of companies and individuals seeking relief. Husbands need to protect themselves and their families from debt.

Allocation of Finances

Husbands should take great care to reach agreement with their wives on each area of financial responsibility and the funds needed by the husband and the wife to carry out their responsibilities. The husband should then be sure that the funds are always available on or before the date scheduled. Being erratic will produce discord and disharmony.

Spiritual Needs

As an individual drove near a large church, he stopped at the traffic light to let church members who had just left their service cross the street. As he watched, he realized that the large majority were women. It was a graphic example of the historic problem in many churches in which men abandon church and leave spiritual leadership to their wives. This was confirmed as he spoke with the pastor of another group about leadership in their church, who said, "Let's face it. It's the women in church who get things done."

The husband was commanded to be the head of the wife (1Corinthians 11:3). This includes the responsibility for spiritual matters as well as physical matters. When husbands take the lead in prayer, Bible study and devotions both at home and in church, it provides a sense of security that the wife needs if she is to function effectively as a wife and mother rather than competing with her husband because he fails to carry out his responsibilities.

Physical Need

Sex 1 Corinthians 7:4 says:

> *The wife's body does not belong to her alone*
> *but also to her husband.*

*In the same way, the husband's body
does not belong to him alone but also to his wife.*

As the natural pursuers and aggressors in sexual matters, husbands seem to need little encouragement about leading in this area. Unfortunately, they may lead abruptly, and miss the subtlety of long-range physical relations that can culminate in enjoyable sexual activity for both sides.

Husbands need to lead in physical matters between husband and wife in areas other than sexual activity. Wives need attention and companionship both *before* and *after* physical union if the *true oneness* spoken of in Ephesians 5:31 and Genesis 2:24 is to become a reality.

Malachi 2:14 discusses "The wife of our youth." When husbands are young and courting, they often provide attention, companionship, flowers, gifts, and romance to capture the girl they want. These must all continue for a lifetime (although probably not with the same white-heat intensity) if we want our marriages to last for a lifetime.

Protection. Rape and assault against women of all ages is becoming rampant in our society. If a wife is truly as her husband's own body and the person who he most cherishes, then he will want to protect her. Husbands should take the responsibility to make their wives as secure as possible. This includes 1) cars that don't break down, 2) traveling with their wives or being sure they have traveling companions, 3) avoiding nighttime travel in dangerous areas, 4) providing secure homes with neighborhood watches, security systems, or other ways in which they can be secure.

Emotional Needs

When a wife determines (often in opposition to the tremendous pressure of society and her own need for fulfillment) to submit herself as a wife and mother in order that strong, lasting families can produce the fruit that God wants, she needs much encouragement. Wives need the same applause, appreciation, and sense of accomplishment that the workplace provides. If women are going to be willing to remain in the role God designed for them as "helpers" and mothers, then that role must be placed back up on the pedestal of honor it held in earlier times.

Future Needs

Leaders have been described as those who see further into the future than others. When Thomas told Jesus that he didn't know where Jesus was going and that he (Thomas) didn't know the way, Jesus responded, "I am the way..." (John 14:5–6) In other words, Jesus seemed to be saying, "Follow me, Thomas. Your direction and security are in me. I hold your future in my hands."

In a sense, wives who follow their husbands are in this same vulnerable position. They look to their husbands not only to provide for today, but for the future. As a result, husbands need to be like Jesus, who said he was going "to prepare a place for you." (John 14:2) They need to prepare and to plan so they can provide for the needs of their wives when the husband is gone or unable to provide.

This means establishing a cash reserve for rainy days that come into every family; life, medical and disability insurance; provision for education and retirement years; wills and trusts; and living wills and written instructions concerning assets and suggestions on how to proceed upon the husband's death or incapacity.

Families, like other institutions, have both internal and external responsibilities. Cities have a mayor (outside) and a city manager (inside). Businesses have sales and public relations (outside) and production and employee relations (inside). Families have husbands who are responsible to provide and to protect from the outside, while the wife securely builds a family from the inside. These responsibilities overlap and are interdependent, but each carries out a primary role while helping the other succeed in his or her primary role. In this way, they *complete* rather than *compete* with one another in their marriage. Again, reversal or abandonment of these assigned roles may give some short-term satisfaction and bring some success in single-parent homes and in the outside institutions of business, church and government, but these may prove to be counterproductive if our goal is lifetime, fruitful, and fulfilling marriages.

B. Increase

But women will be saved through childbearing—
if they continue in faith, love and holiness with propriety.
(1Timothy 2:15)

In the beginning, God made the world and all that is in it. Then He handed it to mankind and told us to increase (Genesis 1:28). This is what happens in fruitful marriages. Husbands begin the process and wives then increase what the husband has begun. Just as we need to be grateful to God for His provision, so should a wife be grateful for that which she receives from her husband and *she needs to tell him so.* The world is often a jungle. A husband survives much better when he is thanked, sincerely and often, for his efforts.

Let's look at some of the areas where wives can increase what their husbands initially provide.

Children

The most basic "increase" is children. The husband provides the seed that is planted in the wife. Her egg then unites with this small deposit. She feeds it, cares for it, and in nine months she brings forth a child.

Biblical Examples The Scriptures are full of examples of Godly women who are extolled and remembered throughout history because they were wives and mothers. Sarah followed her husband Abraham, and in old age she brought forth a child. She and her husband became the mother and father of millions of descendants. Hannah prayed for and then gave back to God's service her son, Samuel, who led and counseled the early Jewish nation. Loyal, dedicated Ruth sought out and submitted to older Boaz to become the great grandmother of King David. Elizabeth was described at length as the mother of John the Baptist. Most revered of all was Mary, the mother of Jesus, who accepted the seed from the Holy Spirit and brought forth the one we call Savior and Lord.

By contrast, only a few women in the Bible (e.g., Judge Deborah in the Old Testament and tentmaker Priscilla in the New Testament) received recognition and a place in God's Word emphasizing their outside careers.

"Nations in Their Wombs" Women in Biblical times—such as Rebekah, who was told she carried whole "nations" in her womb (Genesis 25:23)—were encouraged in their role as wives and

mothers. Today, women are often urged to emphasize their careers, then, if there is time later in life, they can consider having a child or two.

But the inescapable fact is that the future of mankind lies in the wombs of the women of each generation.

Obviously, it takes more than two children for couples to "increase." Yet, much of the industrialized world is producing less than two children per couple, so that many nations are not only not "increasing"—*they are not even reproducing themselves!*

Physical and Spiritual Children This is not to say that all of us should have physical children. Many who are married are unable to have children. Some of these will adopt, others will not. Others, like Paul, remain single and celibate, a role that is also honored and extolled by God (1 Corinthians 7). However, all Christians, whether or not they raise physical children, are to be involved in helping to bring forth and to raise to maturity the family of God (Colossians 1:27–29). The Bible says:

> *Remember this: Whoever sows sparingly*
> *will also reap sparingly,*
> *and whoever sows generously*
> *will also reap generously.*
> (2 Corinthians 9:6)

Each generation must decide for itself what it will sow and reap. If we live only for the current thrill of consumption and winning and receiving recognition in today's world of business, government, sports, and even the formal church, then that's what we will receive. But if we sow and reap both physical and spiritual children, we can someday say with the Psalmist:

> *Sons are a heritage from the Lord, children a reward from him.*
> (Psalm 127:3)

Man's society says, "Compete and consume now," but this produces death when our generation is over. God's society says, "Serve and increase." This produces life and the generations multiply as we were commanded.

Homes
Wives carry on the basic functions of increasing not only in the conception and raising of children, but in all of life. The husband works and provides, and the wife increases for the benefit of the husband, the wife, and their family. Food is turned into meals, cloth into clothing, and a house into a home. In short, wives take all types of seeds that are provided by their husbands, and they produce gardens.

Again, neither of us is independent; we are interdependent. It isn't that wives never produce money or husbands never work at home, but each spouse seems to have a Biblical *primary* role in most fruitful lifetime marriages. How poor the marriage would be if both decide to become the "provider" with the result that neither has the time nor the energy to be the "increaser" and carefully nurture seeds into gardens that the whole family can enjoy.

Proverbs 31 is probably the most concentrated example of a Godly wife and mother. One woman said it made her tired just to read it! It is obviously a composite portrait; a goal that probably is never fully realized by any one wife any more than the composite "lover," of 1 Corinthians 13 that we spoke of earlier, can be fully realized by one individual husband. But both provide excellent specific suggestions to show us better how to live out the roles of husband and wife.

As we read these verses, it is clear that a Godly wife is not a timid, withdrawing underling, but a strong partner in the family enterprise. Listen as she is described:

Verse 10—	She is worth more than rubies.
Verse 11—	She has the full confidence of her husband.
Verse 12—	She brings her husband good, not harm for a lifetime.
Verse 13—	She sews.
Verse 14—	She shops.
Verse 15—	She rises early to provide food and to direct her servants.
Verse 16—	She purchases land and plants.
Verse 17—	She works physically.
Verse 18—	She buys and sells.
Verse 19—	She makes clothing.
Verse 20—	She helps the poor.
Verse 21–22—	She makes clothing and bed coverings for her family.
Verse 23—	Her respected husband is an elder at the city gate.
Verse 24—	She makes and sells clothing to merchants.
Verse 25—	As she works for her family, she is clothed with strength and dignity and she is not afraid of the future.

Verse 26— She speaks with wisdom and faithful instruction.
Verse 27— She is busy as she watches over the affairs of her household.

It seems clear that a wife's work is concentrated at home as she "watches over the affairs of her household..."

In the New Testament, Lydia, before acknowledging Christ, was a "dealer in purple cloth." Obviously, she was a businesswoman. It isn't stated, however, whether she was married, had children, or what she did as her principal occupation after the conversion took place (Acts 16:14). Priscilla was a "tentmaker" with her husband Aquila, and worked for a time with the Apostle Paul (Acts 18:3). Again, it isn't clear whether they had children, nor whether or not this was a home occupation. However, Paul's instruction to Titus, concerning older women's role in training Christian wives *is* clear:

> *Then they can train the younger women to love their husbands*
> *and children, to be self-controlled and pure, to be busy at home,*
> *to be kind, and to be subject to their husbands,*
> *so that no one will malign the work of God.*
> (Titus 2:4–5)

God also gave special instructions and provision for the care of widows (but not of widowers) in both the Old and New Testament (Deuteronomy 14:29; 1 Timothy 5:3–16). This seems to indicate that the principal vocation and means of sustenance of wives (but not husbands) was inside of marriage, since the church and relatives were to care for older widows, and younger widows were to remarry. By contrast, the church today seems largely to have abandoned widows' physical support, just as many husbands have abandoned their wives' physical support. As a result, modern wives, including many Christian wives, are now encouraged to pursue vocations and careers outside the home since there is no provision by the family or the church to care for them when they are widowed. Instead, our society urges women to work outside the home so they themselves can receive additional income now and broader pension and Social Security benefits when they become older or widowed.

This brings us to an interesting question. Can wives, "have it all:" a husband, family, and career during their lifetime? Obviously, none of us can have everything. However, it appears that wives may (if they are patient and do it in tandem) have a husband, then children, then their career.

There do not appear to be Biblical answers to this question. Perhaps we are going to have to look in the future at the examples of Christian marriages in which wives have pursued a later career to determine whether or not later generations were strengthened or damaged in the process.

Step 4

Praise and Glow

A. Praise

Her children arise and call her blessed;
her husband also, and he praises her.
(Proverbs 31:28)

The Standing Ovation
When women *Follow, Respect,* and *Increase* as spelled out in God's Word, men are prompted to "rise up and call them blessed." Perhaps you have wondered about the custom that used to be observed (but which is now considered increasingly archaic in the modern competitive world) in which men and children would rise up when a woman entered the room. However, after we read the work and service this proverbial Godly woman renders for her husband and family, it is easy to understand this custom of past years that marked deep respect for such a wife and mother.

But not only should husbands "rise up" for their wives, they also need to "praise" them. Wives need to be assured often of their husband's love, gratitude, and respect. The work world provides paychecks, perks, service pins, pensions, and other "strokes" to constantly assure workers how much they are valued. There are often exciting people to meet, interesting work to do, and sometimes places to go.

Marriage

By contrast, a career as a wife and mother can appear and actually become somewhat drab, lonely, and unrewarding. Recently at a business dinner meeting, I listened as two young professional women discussed the role of motherhood versus their outside careers. One shared how she was eagerly looking forward to getting a "nanny" for her new child so she could return to work. Both readily agreed that the work world was far easier and more attractive than "staying at home with the kids."

No longer does the world suggest that being a wife and mother is a worthwhile, lifelong career. No longer is it enough to be a wife serving her husband and children so that they may succeed. Now the goal, in many Christian as well as non-Christian homes, is for the wife to succeed in a career outside the home. Fathers and mothers proudly proclaim their daughters' college degrees and working titles—while the divorce statistics continue to climb.

As society increasingly encourages outside careers for both sons and daughters as the chief purpose and goal in life, the role of wife and mother deteriorates further. Marriages are delayed. Casual living arrangements between men and women increase. Homosexuality is increasingly alleged as normative. Childbearing is delayed, often until the late thirties, which leaves little time for raising a family of any size. Families continue to shrink and God's command to multiply is thwarted as we "chase the wind" of outside careers. By contrast, too few of us praise the career of wife and mother that has no degree or title placed on it by the world.

In earlier years, "Mother of the Year" was a coveted front page award. Today, it seldom makes the news on any page. If the Christian community truly believes that God has a wonderful, unique, and satisfying role for wives and mothers, then girls and women must be assured of this at every occasion. In Bible times, it was a mark of God's great favor when women were granted children. While women were seldom extolled in Scriptures for being leaders or carrying on outside careers, Godly women were praised throughout God's Word for their careers as wives and mothers. This Biblical practice should be continued today.

Ways to Praise
We all like to receive praise for a job well done. It spurs us on to greater effort. Some time ago I heard an employee tell her employer, "You're going to work me to death if you don't stop telling me what a great job I'm doing."

Wives, too, want and need to be assured their role has eternal significance and that it is respected and appreciated. Here are some of the specific ways this can be done:

Wedding Anniversaries If marriage is the entrance into a woman's most significant role in life, it needs to be commemorated and never overlooked. Special events, cards, and gifts are a constant reminder that the husband and family consider marriage of extreme importance, and each year this should be a heightened experience, far more important than company recognition for years of service she might receive if she were employed outside the home. Such wedding anniversaries proclaim to the world that this is a lifetime union.

Gifts Remembrances remind a wife that she is not forgotten. She is appreciated. She is special. Children need to be taught not simply to receive, but to give. As they see husbands praise, recognize, and give to their mothers, so will these children learn to expect this kind of atmosphere when they are grown. For some reason, jewelry often seems special to a woman. Perhaps it proclaims to her that she truly is "worth far more than rubies" when the "rubies" are given to her.

Homes Wives make a house into a home. As wives carefully nurture flowers and other living plants and provide curtains, furnishings, and other items of beauty both inside and outside the home, it becomes apparent how drab life would be without their loving touch. Wives need to be encouraged and praised, not scolded, for money, time, and effort spent in homemaking. Jesus's commendation to the woman who poured the expensive ointment on him made it clear that doing something "beautiful" for God pleases Him (Mark 14:6). When a Godly wife provides beauty for her family, she surely is doing it also for God and pleasing both. If a woman can be fulfilled by a career decorating other people's homes and receive praise for her work, but she never receives praise for the work she does within her own home, why wouldn't she want an outside career?

Meals Recently at a church retreat, panel members were asked about family traditions they felt were important. One of the panelists pointed out the deterioration of most modern mealtimes and the chilling effect this is having on the family. In this age of "fast food" and separate careers, we see husbands, wives, and children who often eat alone or with others outside the family. When at home, each person often makes exactly what he or she individually wants, and then eats alone at the counter or in front of the TV without speaking.

What a difference from the old-time family meal! There is no tradition more significant in maintaining family life than families gathered around a meal table for good food and fellowship. First we learn *submission* as we eat what we are given. Next we learn *togetherness* as we speak and listen to one another. Finally, we learn *gratefulness* as we thank God for His overall provision, the father for providing and the mother for increasing into the meal that we enjoy together with the fellowship of a family gathered together in a loving and caring relationship.

Husbands need to praise their wives when they take the lead in carrying out their difficult tasks day after day.

The list of items for which wives should be praised goes on and on. One good method is to use the checklist on page 62 showing the activities of the proverbial Godly woman in Proverbs 31. After each of these items, husbands should say, *"Praise her!"*

Winning Words
Many husbands find it difficult to verbalize praise for their wives. Words often seem awkward and almost insincere. Yet, it is essential if the role of wife and mother is to be encouraged and increased. Too often, men can be like the reticent husband who, when pressed, told his wife in exasperation, "I told you I loved you when I married you, and if I stop loving you, I'll tell you that, too."

If lifetime marriages are to continue, husbands need to praise their wives for the Godly work they perform. No man, woman, or child should have any doubt that followers of Christ consider the role of wife and mother of eternal significance and that we praise this career for women above and beyond any competitive career the world has to offer. It has been said that men are reached through their eyes and women through their ears. It is not enough, therefore, simply to show wives that they are loved. They must be praised verbally!

B. Glow

> *...and to present her to himself as a*
> *radiant church, without stain or wrinkle*
> *or any other blemish, but holy and blameless.*
> (Ephesians 5:27)

Don't Distract with Verbal Noise
While it may be difficult for many husbands to speak out, it is sometimes difficult for some wives not to speak! Listen the next time you ride in an automobile with two or three couples to determine who carries the conversation.

Peter cautioned wives that their husbands are often won through their eyes, not their ears:

> *Wives, in the same way be submissive to your husbands*
> *so that, if any of them do not believe the word,*
> *they may be won over without words by the behavior of their wives,*
> *when they see the purity and reverence of your lives.*
> (1 Peter 3:1–2)

It is so tempting for wives (because they, themselves, seem often motivated by words) to use words in an effort to motivate or change their husbands. However, to a man (who can often be motivated more through his eyes than his ears), such wifely pleas may become mere nagging.

Wives who attempt to persuade or motivate their husbands by their words are often ineffective. *A careful review of the proverbial Godly woman in Proverbs 31 reveals that she engages in works versus words by a ratio of twelve to one!* And the only reference to her words reflects that she uses her tongue very carefully when she speaks:

> *She speaks with wisdom,*
> *and faithful instruction is on her tongue.*
> (Proverbs 31:26)

When her husband then praises her, it is not because of her conversation (or her beauty), but because of her God-centered attitude and actions:

> *Many women do noble things, but you surpass them all.*
> *Charm is deceptive, and beauty is fleeting;*
> *but a woman who fears the Lord is to be praised.*
> *Give her the reward she has earned, and let her works bring her praise*
> *at the city gate.*
> (Proverbs 31:29–31)

Prayer and Prophecy
The Bible makes it clear that many women have been gifted in the ministries of prayer and prophecy (Exodus 15:20; Acts 21:8–9; 1 Corinthians 11:5). But the Bible also seems to draw a

distinction between prayer and prophecy as opposed to teaching and exercising authority over men. When women take on this latter role, husbands often feel encouraged to abdicate from their responsibility of leading and speaking out. Paul instructs Timothy that this should not be, as he says:

> *A woman should learn in quietness and full submission.*
> *I do not permit a woman to teach or to have authority*
> *over a man; she must be silent.*
> (1Timothy 2:11–12)

He then explains why women should practice the art of submission and quietness as he concludes:

> *For Adam was formed first, then Eve.*
> *And Adam was not the one deceived;*
> *it was the woman who was deceived and became a sinner.*
> (1Timothy 2:13–14)

This is a hard teaching. It goes against the grain, particularly in the modern scene. However, God's ways often seem contrary to man's ways and we often believe that our natural instincts are right. But Proverbs 14:12 warns us:

> *There is a way that seems right to a man,*
> *but in the end it leads to death.*

If our goal is to build strong Biblical lifetime marriages that will also be Godly examples to future generations, then we need to carry out the words of Scripture, not our own natural inclinations. Just as husbands have the hard task of learning to *Lead,*

Love, Provide, and *Praise* their wives, so wives need to learn the difficult response of quietly *Glowing,* after they have learned to *Follow, Respect,* and *Increase* what their husbands provide.

God is in the business of transforming us into His image. Wives who develop a quiet inner beauty, accompanied by Godly works, can and do have a profound effect on their husbands, children, and others far more than they affect them by their words alone.

Don't Distract with Visual Noise
Did you ever buy a diamond? Do you remember how the jeweler made the sale? First, he carefully unfurled a piece of black velvet. Then he dramatically laid a gem carefully and deliberately on the cloth. It sparkled and shown in all its brilliance—solitary, beautiful, almost awesome in quiet splendor.

By contrast, look sometime in a variety store window where cheap articles are displayed. They are surrounded by tinsel and cheapness. A diamond would be lost and never seen nor appreciated in this kind of setting. Surely the same analogy holds true with wives. Satan always has a substitute for God's commands and provisions. In this case, Satan's substitute seems to be for women to use artificial tinsel and gaudiness rather than Godly femininity in an effort to be seen and get man's attention. But God's genuine women are like jewels who reflect the quiet beauty of the inner spirit. Paul writes to Timothy:

> *I also want women to dress modestly, with decency and propriety,*
> *not with braided hair or gold or pearls or expensive clothes,*
> *but with good deeds, appropriate for women who profess to worship God.*
> (1Timothy 2:9–10)

God is not a killjoy. He isn't attempting to make women drab and unattractive. Instead, he wants their *true* beauty to be seen. This can't happen if they are overshadowed by gaudy clothes and excessive jewelry. God wants us to hear the pure music of their lives, not to be visually distracted that we miss the inner beauty. Peter said it this way:

> *Your beauty should not come from outward adornment,*
> *such as braided hair and the wearing of gold jewelry and fine clothes.*
> *Instead, it should be that of your inner self,*
> *the unfading beauty of a gentle and quiet spirit,*
> *which is of great worth in God's sight.*
> (1 Peter 3:3–4)

"Radiant"—"Without Spot or Wrinkle"

Paul, in Ephesians 5:27, notes that the church, as the wife of Christ, is to be "radiant." This is also true of earthly wives. How it pleases women when they glow as a radiant bride, and how a loving husband is thrilled and pleased by this beautiful, radiant woman he presents to himself "without spot or wrinkle or any other blemish."

This is an important point. The modern trend is to try to be wrinkle-free, spot-free and blemish-free all our lives. Physically, we use vanishing cream and facelifts to try to beautify our dying physical bodies. Without discussing the merits of this kind of holding action, it seems important that we hear the following spiritual truth recounted by a man in his later years:

> "When I was a youngster I noticed my father had wrinkles, small black and brown spots, and other blemishes

on his skin. Now, I look and see that I have them, and so does my wife. But if I see the beauty of my wife through her quiet inner spirit, she is wrinkle-free, spotless, and without any blemish."

"If we depend upon physical attraction and youthful beauty, then the longer we live together, the less attractive our wives (and ourselves) become. But, if we look at their quiet inner spirit, they can become radiant and beautiful, without any wrinkle, spot, or blemish. And I can tell you that after more than forty years of marriage, my wife is more beautiful to me today than at any time in her life. In fact, even her physical face and form, have a beauty that comes from her works, which praise her and form her quiet inner spirit that deeply and overwhelmingly pleasure me."

Be a Jewel
It seems appropriate that a Christian wife should be referred to as a "jewel." After all, she is "worth far more than rubies" (Proverbs 31:10).

"But remember," said a participant in a conference discussing the roles of husband and wife, "a jewel has no internal light of its own. Instead, it reflects the light that shines upon it."

If a wife is to glow and become radiant, and in so doing please herself and those around her, she must, figuratively speaking, reflect the light from her husband's love and attention. When husbands and wives *compete* with one another at any level, the light of marriage sometimes seems to grow dim—and too often grow completely dark. What a waste!

By contrast, there is nothing so satisfying to wives, husbands, their children, friends, and society as the *glow* of a Godly wife showing forth the radiance of true Christian marriage!

III. The Walk

Whoever claims to live in Him must walk as Jesus did.
(1 John 2:6)

If we are to enjoy good, lifelong marriages, husbands and wives should strive not only to carry out their own unique roles, but also to walk together under the Lordship of Christ into the oneness He has prepared for them. Together, a husband and wife can form something of beauty before God and man.

We have listed four simple but awesome steps that can help husbands and wives "complete" rather than "compete" with one another:

HUSBAND	WIFE
Lead	Follow
Love	Respect
Provide	Increase
Praise	Glow

As each partner faithfully walks through these steps, the marriage seems to become a living entity as shown by the following illustration:

- In your mind, draw an arrow from *Lead* to *Follow*, for until a husband leads, a wife cannot follow.
- Next, draw an arrow from *Follow* to *Love*, showing that when the wife follows, it causes her husband to look around and see this woman placing herself under his

protection, which brings forth in him a love and willingness to give himself up for her.
- Then draw an arrow from *Love* to *Respect*, showing that when the husband loves and gives himself up for his wife, it brings forth her respect for him as a husband.
- Next, draw an arrow from *Respect* to *Provide*, because a husband who looks around and sees his wife following and respecting him, usually wants to provide for and protect her as his cherished bride.
- Once he provides physically and spiritually for his wife, she can then increase what he has begun, so draw an arrow from *Provide* to *Increase*.
- After she increases what her husband provides, it brings forth his praise for her Godly works, so draw an arrow from *Increase* to *Praise*.
- Finally, as he praises her, she becomes a radiant bride, so draw an arrow from *Praise* to *Glow*.

When these steps are followed it looks like this:

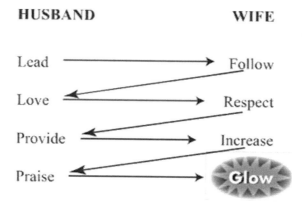

No longer are these two competing individuals. Instead, by "submit(ting) to one another..." (Ephesians 5:21), and carrying out their biblical roles, such a husband and wife have so integrated their lives that they truly have become "one flesh." As a result, God is glorified, the partners receive joy and fulfillment, and society and future generations are blessed.

This brings, us, however, to the final question we have silently asked ourselves throughout this discussion:

How do we, as fallible, but sincere, followers of Christ, successfully walk through these steps in order to reach our goal of "oneness?"

IV. The Hope

For it is by grace you have been saved...
(Ephesians 2:8)

At the beginning of this discussion, we observed that no one was perfect, that two imperfect people could not make a perfect marriage, and that good, lifetime marriages seemed to flow from the grace of God and the application of His Word. We have discussed at length God's Word and its application. This is our goal, and we need to work toward building marriages that are as perfect as possible. But we are, and will always be—until we join our Lord in Heaven—imperfect. Therefore, let's conclude by discussing God's grace in marriage.

For reasons only He knows, God has chosen to work through frail, imperfect men and women to carry out His perfect will. Abraham lied about his wife and half-sister, Sarah, to protect himself, but became the father of millions. Jacob, the deceiver, became Israel, the father of a holy nation. Moses, the murderer, became the leader chosen by God to lead Israel out of Egypt. David, after having been chosen by God, committed adultery with Bathsheba and then arranged to have her husband killed in order to cover his sin. The Apostle Paul, before his conversion, joined in the killing of Stephen, the first Christian martyr. And Peter, after his conversion and three years walking with Jesus, denied his Lord three times.

None of us will be able to perform perfectly our roles in life, including the role of husband or wife. But despite our frailties and failures, by God's grace, His great work can be done through us.

Some of us will find certain areas discussed above manageable and other areas will be very difficult. What is easy for one may be difficult or almost impossible for another. But we can be sure of this: God's grace is sufficient to make marriages wholesome and good, even though rungs in these four-step ladders we have discussed are broken or even missing!

One wife, after years of praying for God to change her husband in a particular area, finally cried out in desperation, "Please God, if you won't change him, then change me!"

Sometime later, her husband came to her and asked her to pray that he would change—in the exact area of her frustration!

God can change us. He can also change our marriage partners. Often He changes both of us by sharpening each of us through the other.

He knows our hearts. I don't believe His final goal is perfect marriages—but perfected people! Even if a marriage fails, that still is not the end. God is in the business of bringing beauty out of ashes. Just as we have watched God redeem the lives of His saints such as Abraham, Jacob, Moses, David, Paul, and Peter, so will He redeem us, if we are willing. This may be through a wholesome and good marriage (which obviously is what we would prefer), but it may also be out of the ashes of a broken marriage. But it will only happen if we follow Him and abide by His Word!

So whatever your circumstances and challenges may be, remember this: God loves us. He will care for us and help us to be and to do what He has planned if we submit to Him and follow Him throughout our lives. He says to us today, as He did to His prophet Jeremiah:

> *"For I know the plans I have for you," declares the Lord,*
> *"plans to prosper you and not to harm you,*
> *plans to give you hope and a future.*
> *Then you will call upon me and come and*
> *pray to me, and I will listen to you.*
> *You will seek me and find me when you seek me with all your heart."*
> (Jeremiah 29:11–13)

Part III
Sixty Years of Marriage

There is a time for everything,
and a season for every activity under heaven:
a time to be born and a time to die…
He has made everything beautiful in its time…
(Ecclesiastes 3:1–2a, 11a)

A Personal Note

2008

Someone who recently read an earlier version of Part I, "Why Marriage," said to me quite candidly: "I was so excited to read about the ideal for marriage, but I was terribly disappointed that you didn't tell us what had worked to make your marriage beautiful for you."

I decided the reproof was well founded. I am not a marriage counselor, but, as a follower of Jesus, I am commanded to be a witness for Him (Matthew 28:19–20; Acts 1:8). And that surely must include passing on some of what we see, hear, and experience in marriage.

So what is written here is the "rest of the story," concentrating on lessons we learned as we tried to apply God's Word to our marriage. I realize now that this later material could not have been written when we wrote "Why Marriage?" in 1992. We needed the additional sixteen years of older married life to bring into focus what we were experiencing in the earlier years.

Ellie and I met in college in 1946 and were married on August 28, 1948. She was twenty-one years old, and I was twenty-three. Now she is eighty-one and I am eighty-three. I am aware that a lot of information from our sixty years of marriage is packed into the next few pages. As I once heard an overwhelmed man exclaim, "It is a little like trying to get a drink out of a fire hydrant!" However, since each example speaks to an issue that arose during our marriage years, we opted to keep them all. Hopefully, readers will go through them slowly, (perhaps as couples if they are married or considering marriage) and then decide for themselves what is meaningful for their lives.

Remember, we all err—so, as always, hold on to what is good (of God)—discard the rest.

From Grandpa With Love

Sixty Years of Marriage

The following comments are not intended as a model for a "beautiful marriage," but rather as contents of a "Recipe Box" or a "Tool Box" containing some of the concepts gradually accumulated through the years out of much trial and error, which have enhanced and strengthened our marriage. These experiences and conclusions have been helpful for us. We hope they will be helpful for you—but that must be your decision.

Keep in mind we can learn some things from others, but much we must work out in our own lives. As I chided (with a chuckle) a younger man who said he wanted what I now had, "You want what I have—you just don't want the forty years in between!" It is hard work, but it is worth it!

A. Being "Under God"

Marriage is a Gift from God.
By far the most fundamental reality in marriage is that it is a gift of God. We don't create marriage or oneness; we are simply stewards of what we are given. The Bible says:

> ...what God has joined together, let man not separate.
> (Matthew 19:6)

We do not become "one" by our efforts after we marry; instead we receive "oneness" from God when we marry. And the Bible makes it clear that:

> *...it is required that those who have been given a trust must prove faithful."*
> (1 Corinthians 4:2)

Our job is to hold onto this gift of oneness and not lose it or destroy it—and to recover it if we lose it for a time!

Join the Family of God
Most of us get our concepts of marriage from our parents and our culture. But, all these are fallible (Romans 3:23). If we want a Godly marriage, we first need to be born again and join the family of God (John 3:1–8).

After struggling for years, Ellie and I both asked Jesus into our lives. I believe it is a necessary step for everyone who wants a marriage patterned after "Christ and the church."

Use God's Instructions for God's Gift
Marriage became much more enjoyable and workable when we began to follow God's instructions in the Bible, rather than relying on the wisdom of the world.

Studying the Bible about any subject takes time and effort, but it is worthwhile. If we want to know about money, study money. If we want to know about law, study law. If we want to know how to have a beautiful marriage, study to see what the Bible says, watch Godly marriages, and get all the Godly counsel we can.

B. Personal Actions

Marriage is a Lot of Giving.
The Kingdom of God is often right side up from the upside-down world in which we live. So we are instructed that "...there are those who are last who will be first, and first who will be last" Luke 13:30); "...whoever loses his life for me will save it" (Luke 9:24); we should take the "lowest place" at the table (Luke 14:10); and "...whoever wants to become great among you must be your servant..." (Matthew 20:26).

The first and foremost place we need to give, and give, and give is in our marriage.

Words, Attitude, and Tone of Voice Are Important.
An important verse, for a good marriage relationship, is:

> *Everyone should be quick to listen,*
> *slow to speak and slow to become angry...*
> (James 1:19b)

A companion verse is found in Proverbs 15:1:

> *A gentle answer turns away wrath,*
> *but a harsh word stirs up anger.*

If we love someone, why would we not listen to them; why would we speak harshly to them; why would we become easily angered; and why would we want to stir up anger in them?

Ask God to Change Me—He Might Change Us Both
One of our great breakthroughs came when Ellie cried:

> "All right, Lord!
> If you won't change him, then change me!"

Instead, God changed us both!

Giving Up Control
Like many of our generation, I felt responsible to control my family. I didn't understand the difference between command and leadership. Command relies on force to control others. Leadership relies on love to win others, so they want to follow us voluntarily (John 13:12–17).

The key is to give control to God and follow Him. When we follow Jesus, it makes it easier for others to follow us.

Being Content
The Apostle, Paul, wrote:

> *I have learned the secret of being content*
> *in any and every situation, whether well fed or hungry,*
> *whether living in plenty or in want.*
> (Philippians 4:12b)

One of the hallmarks of a beautiful marriage is enjoying what we do have, and not complaining about what we don't!

"Choose Thy Love and Love Thy Choice"
Those words appear on a needlepoint wall hanging made for one of our children. It is a good reminder when the honeymoon is over and reality sets in. Our spouses usually don't change too much; we just get to know them better.

In our society, we have the great privilege of choosing our mate. It behooves us to make the choice carefully and then to endure the hard times that all marriages encounter. Romans 5:3–5 was a key verse for us and helped us persevere during difficult circumstances:

> *Not only so, but we also rejoice in our sufferings,*
> *because we know that suffering produces*
> *perseverance; perseverance, character;*
> *and character, hope. And hope does not disappoint us,*
> *because God has poured his love into our hearts by the Holy Spirit,*
> *whom he has given us.*

"Why, Mary Loves the Lamb You Know"
It took me a long time to learn that we have to receive love before we can give it to others. Two things helped me understand. One was a nursery rhyme Ellie often quoted in our home:

> "Why does the lamb love Mary so?" the eager children cry.
> "Why, Mary loves the lamb you know,"
> the teacher did reply.

I also read 1 John 4:19, which explained:

> *We love because he (God) first loved us.*

When we learn to let God and our spouse love us, it humbles us—but it also starts a domino effect that makes marriage a never-ending love affair.

Our Most Valuable Treasure
Some question whether wives were valued in Old Testament times. I believe they were. Isaac sent a servant with ten camels carrying "gold and silver jewelry and articles of clothing" (Genesis 24, especially verse 53) that were given to Rebekah and her family before she became his wife. Jacob worked seven (then seven more) years to earn Rachel:

> *...but they seemed like only a few days to him*
> *because of his love for her.*
> (Genesis 29:16–30 especially verse 20)

Our spouse is our most precious treasure. We spend much of our lives with and for them. It pays big dividends in marital happiness, when we show and tell each other, *often,* how much we value, enjoy and love them.

Am I a Fool or a Wise Person?
The book of Proverbs often speaks of the contrast between a fool and a wise person. Many have found it rewarding to read one chapter of this book each day of the month for several months. It will not only speak directly to the marriage relationship, but

also instruct us about numerous areas of life that will make our marriages more beautiful.

If we want a beautiful marriage, I recommend spending time in this timeless book. It will enhance a life and a marriage.

Keeping Our Word
If we want a good relationship with anyone, they must be able to count on what we say. Ecclesiastes 5:5 advises:

> *It is better not to vow*
> *than to make a vow and not fulfill it.*

Psalm 15:4 commends a person "who keeps his oath even when it hurts…" When we make a habit of always doing what we say we will do, including our day-to-day promises and commitments, we build trust and enhance our marriage. When we break our word, (often because it is more convenient or advantageous to us) it devalues our partner and brings a separation between husband and wife that is hard to overcome.

If we say we'll be home for dinner (or prepare it) by 6:00 p.m., then *do it!*

Humble Yourselves—Under God's Mighty Hand
Pride is one of our great enemies (Proverbs 6:16). God condemns pride and praises humility (Proverbs 29:23). Sadly, we (particularly we men) often reverse the two because we are motivated by the rewards, medals, and fame offered by the world.

One of the greatest tools for a beautiful marriage is a humble spirit (1 Peter 5:5–6). It may not make us great in the world—but it makes us great in the eyes of our loved ones.

Forgiving
The "Lord's Prayer" (Matthew 6:9–15) tells us to ask God to:

> *Forgive us our debts,*
> *as we also have forgiven our debtors…*

and then warns us:

> *For if you forgive men when they sin against you,*
> *your heavenly Father will also forgive you.*
> *But if you do not forgive men their sins,*
> *your Father will not forgive your sins.*

Human forgiveness benefits the person who gives it as much or more than the person who receives it. It relieves the one forgiven, but it releases the forgiver from all bitterness and spirit of revenge. When we fail to forgive, it puts us in a prison, because our mind is centered on our being wronged. But when we forgive, and then add something good for the wrongdoer, we both benefit. As the Bible says:

> *If your enemy is hungry, feed him; if he is thirsty,*
> *give him something to drink. In doing this,*
> *you will heap burning coals on his head.*
> (Romans 12:20)

Being willing to humble ourselves and ask for forgiveness, and forgiving the other one when we are wronged, are two of the most important tools for a beautiful marriage.

Divorce Was Not An Option
In Malachi 2:16, God announced, "I hate divorce." Other scriptures, however, sometimes allow it (Matthew 19:9; 1 Corinthians 7:10–16). After witnessing the effect of divorce, and handling the heartbreak of divorce cases as a young lawyer, I knew divorce was not for me.

I still remember the day I was standing at the window in our breakfast room and said, "Divorce is not an option for me." I don't know what occasioned the remark, but I learned later from a friend that it made a lasting impression on Ellie.

It takes courage to get married, and it takes effort to stay married in today's permissive environment and easy no-fault divorce laws. We need all the support we can get from our faith, our family, and like-minded friends.

It strengthened us both when divorce was not an option—and we both knew it.

C. Togetherness

Wanting to Be with You
Everyone needs to feel loved and wanted. When I asked one of our daughters how we know if someone loves us, she answered without hesitation, "If they want to be with you."

When Jesus began his ministry He chose twelve to "be with Him" (Mark 3:14). Relationships grow as we spend time together. It not only builds love, it demonstrates that love exists. At one time I tried to chart my daily schedule to try and get a balance. It only showed how off balance I had become—especially when Ellie commented wryly, "How come I get all the nighttime hours?"

Spending time with someone we love and who loves us is a privilege and not a duty. It makes both of us know we are loved.

Carrying Out Our Biblical Roles

Genesis 1 opens with the story of creation including verse 27:

> *So God created man in his own image,*
> *in the image of God he created him;*
> *male and female he created them.*

Husbands and wives each have their own roles in marriage. We were created to *complete* one another, not *compete* against one another. (See Part II "Complete—Don't Compete.") As we carry out our Biblical roles, there is harmony. When one tries to play both roles, or to usurp the role of the other, it just doesn't work as well.

Worshiping Together

Jesus (who was later quoted by Abraham Lincoln around the time of the Civil War) predicted failure for:

> *A house divided against itself...*
> (Luke 11:17)

During years of practicing law, I also discovered that a house that is *divided* (even though not divided against itself) gets paralyzed and simply won't go anywhere.

Ephesians 4:5–6 reminds us there is:

> *...one Lord, one faith, one baptism; one God and Father of all, who is over all and through all and in all.*

Marrying within the same faith; acknowledging and praying to the same God; attending and worshiping in the same church community; and reading and following the same Word of God was a key element in developing strength in our marriage.

Agreeing Together
Jesus told His disciples:

> *Again, I tell you that if two of you on earth agree about anything you ask for, it will be done for you by my Father in Heaven.*
> (Matthew 18:19)

Once a couple begins life together, it doesn't take long to see the wisdom of both agreeing on major decisions affecting the marriage. Men and women are like two sides of a coin—one yet two. We think and see differently, but we usually need both views if we want all that God has waiting for us.

Waiting until we reach agreement is slower, and it requires that we communicate, including listening as well as talking, but the results are usually better—and so is the marriage!

Rejoicing Together and Mourning Together
The Bible instructs us:

> *Rejoice with those who rejoice;*
> *mourn with those who mourn.*
> (Romans 12:15)

Good news—including the "Good News" of the Gospel—is not for hoarding but for sharing. When our mate rejoices with us, it doubles the joy for both. But nothing spoils a day faster than pouring cold water on their smile or laughter.

When sorrow comes, there is often nothing we can do but to share that, also. When our partner grieves with us, it cuts the load in half. It helps just to know someone cares. It hurts terribly to realize that they don't.

Laughter and sorrow are a big part of life—especially when we share them with one another.

Living Together
As we have aged, we often find ourselves saying to one another:

> "I sure like living with you!"

I have no idea when I finally realized that so much of marriage was simply being together no matter where we were or what we were doing. As one man explained to me, "Home is where your wife is!"

It appears God places a desire for companionship in us to draw us first to Himself and then to one another. It is somewhat like physical laws that cause particles of matter to be drawn together and keep the earth from flying apart and the solar system operating in its orderly fashion.

The most complete form of human companionship is a man and woman living together as Husband and Wife—and all that a lifetime of that relationship entails.

Building Memories Together

> *I thank my God every time I remember you.*
> (Philippians 1:3)

Remembering is one of God's great gifts. Our lives become richer and stronger as we recall together the good times we have shared and the hard times that have brought us perseverance, character, and hope (Romans 5:3–5): acknowledging wedding anniversaries; revisiting our honeymoon site and other special places we have shared; observing births followed by birthday celebrations year after year; listening together to songs we have enjoyed; telling and retelling stories that grow into family legends; reviewing movies and pictures of our wedding and other events over the years; rereading old letters, or Bible verses or clippings; and trimming the Christmas tree year after year with ornaments that bring recollections of earlier times.

These are just a few of the ways that memories build our marriages richer and stronger year after year.

Loving One Another
The Apostle Paul specifically instructed husbands to:

> *...love your wives just as Christ loved the church*
> *and gave Himself up for her.*
> (Ephesians 5:25)

The key is giving up what we want and trying to meet our partner's needs. I found that when we do, we are loved greatly in return.

Books are written about the many ways we give and receive love. When we can't tell which one is best—just do all the Godly ones and we will hit the mark!

Liking One Another
One of our little granddaughters often told us "I 'wike' you and I 'wuv' you." She understood early in life there was a difference. As she grew older, her words were, "I like you and I love you," but the distinction remained the same.

Love is what we do; like is what we feel. When I love someone, it means "giving myself up" for them. If I like someone, simply the thought of them gives me pleasure.

It is important that we like, i.e., take pleasure in our spouse. Sometimes because they make us smile or laugh; because we experience a rush of good feelings when we see their face or hear their voice; the way they walk or talk; or we witness a kindness they pour out on someone (perhaps me) who doesn't deserve it.

Now we often say to one another, "I like you and I love you"—or even, "I 'wike' you and I 'wuv' you!" It is amazing how good it makes both of us feel!

D. Children, Extended Families, and Friends

Raising Children
Looking back, it seems that nothing makes marriage more natural and more beautiful than raising children. It forges us together in a way that nothing else can do. And dreams of future generations encourage us through present difficulties.

I know that children are not for everyone. I'm pleased they were for us. Raising five children and later welcoming a nephew who came to live with us, brought us together in a totally unique way.

Extending Our Families
Genesis 2:24 states:

> *For this reason a man will leave his father and mother*
> *and be united to his wife, and they will become one flesh.*

As we spoke with a group of younger married couples, it became clear that many of the wives felt threatened by their husband's latent attachment to their mothers. Some children don't want to leave—and some parents don't want to let go.

Helping married children is a great privilege, as long as both sides recognize that the young ones need to stay connected to, but not controlled by, their parents.

Old family groupings are great memories, but we have to let go and allow new generations to form new chapters in life. In order for marriage to reach its fullest potential, each generation needs to find its own way and cement relationships to one another as they do so.

But, for us, the great privilege of looking around at children, grandchildren, and now great grandchildren brings a satisfaction and sense of purpose that nothing else can provide.

Having Friends
Friends are essential for healthy marriages. We have found our best friend is each other, then other family members. I believe we also need other friends, especially if we are away from our family. (Proverbs 27:10)

And they need to be healthy friends, who build, not destroy, others. We need to avoid what one man called the "marriage wreckers." As 1 Corinthians 15:33b warns:

> *Bad company corrupts good character.*

I am grateful God brought into our life a number of good friendships, some of which have lasted over sixty years. Many of them have been grounded in our mutual relationship as followers of Jesus, which makes them doubly valuable.

It takes effort to establish and keep worthwhile friendships—but it is part of what makes a beautiful marriage.

Conclusion

I suppose everyone has their own description of a beautiful marriage, and how we can best experience it. The suggestions that are described above have worked for us. Hopefully, they can also be helpful for you.

Some time ago, we mentioned in a Bible study that Isaiah 59:21 was a beautiful verse for a family. Later, one of the couples found an original King James page containing that verse and generously passed it on to us. We now keep it in our den (along with a modern version) as a reminder of our responsibility to pass on that which God entrusts to us to those who are following. The NIV says it this way:

> *"As for me, this is my covenant with them,"*
> *says the Lord. "My Spirit, who is on you,*
> *and my words that I have put in your mouth*
> *will not depart from your mouth,*
> *or from the mouths of your children,*
> *or from the mouths of their descendants*
> *from this time on and forever," says the Lord.*

Surely there are no more important words to pass on than those relating to our faith and a Godly marriage.

Grandma and I pray that those of you who are called to marriage will have a long and fruitful relationship—and that you will look back at the end of your journey, content that you have walked with God and that your marriage truly has been a *beautiful mystery*, patterned after the union of "Christ and the church!"

From Grandpa With Love

Part IV

Who Determines the Time to Leave?

From one man he made every nation of men, that they should inhabit the whole earth; and he determined the times set for them and the exact places where they should live.
(Acts 17:26)

Preface

Spring of 2009

As the years have gone by, I have heard an increasing number of questions raised about the end of life, e.g.:

- "Why do we have to live so long if we can't enjoy life?"
- "Isn't it all right to end suffering?"
- "Are we being good stewards of our individual and collective resources, if we use up assets supporting the life of old people who can never get better?"
- "Why shouldn't we be like the oldsters in ancient societies, who simply walked off and died?"

Recently the questions have come in such rapid fire succession that I decided God was telling me to think through the issue, so that I could make an informed decision for myself and also pass on my personal conclusions to others.

Because of dramatic advances in the field of medicine and related sciences, we are now able to prolong life by extraordinary but sometimes artificial means. We are also able to terminate life with increasing ease. As a result, end of life issues have become increasingly complicated. We find ourselves dealing with Living Wills, DNRs (Do Not Resuscitate Orders), application (or refusal) of possible treatment, and sometimes conflicting opinions from a variety of medical, religious, and legal experts. In addition, because of third party payers such as insurance companies and the government, we increasingly hear of managed care and rationed care being imposed on individuals who have lost control of what options they can and should have.

Although the subject is an uncomfortable one, I concluded it was better to meet the issue now, since the end approaches for us all, and we make better decisions when they are reasoned and thoughtful rather than in the heat and stress of the moment.

As a result I have made my own decisions about what specific documents and directives to sign. But those actions (or inactions) were really an outgrowth of the underlying, fundamental question we all must answer:

> "Shall man or God
> decide when our race here on earth is over?"

Once we decide who is ultimately in charge, the application of the other options available in each individual case fall more easily into place.

For me, the answer to the question is,

> "God—not man!"

On the following pages I will attempt to give you reasons why I have come to that conclusion. My comments are not meant as advice or counsel to others, but rather as one man's attempt to tell what the Scriptures have said to me about one of the most important decisions any of us will ever make.

Remember, we all err. So, test what I say, hold onto what is good (of God)—and discard the rest.

From Grandpa With Love

Who Determines the Time to Leave?

God creates us and decides everything about us, including when we shall be born. We are not in control of our creation, birth, or early years. But as we grow and mature many of us gradually take control of our lives. Hopefully, at some point we realize the need to surrender our will to God and be born again into His Eternal Kingdom. When that happens, he calls us to give control back to Him and "become like little children" (Matthew 18:3). From that point on, we pray the Lord's Prayer:

> *Our Father in heaven, hallowed be your name,*
> *your kingdom come,*
> ***your will*** *be done on earth as it is in heaven.*
> (Matthew 6:9–10. Emphasis added.)

Thereafter, we are to seek *God's* will, not ours—and that would seem to include letting Him choose the time, place, and circumstances of our death, just as He earlier chose the time, place, and circumstances of our birth.

Unfortunately, Satan has promised since the Garden of Eden that if we obey him, we can "be like God." But we can't. And when we try and take control of our own destiny, we end up failing. What a tragedy, to be created by God, and then demand that *our* will determine when and how we shall die—like Saul (1 Samuel 9:15–16 and 1 Samuel 31:4) or Judas! (Luke 6:13–16 and Matthew 27:5).

It is important to finish well. Jesus pointed out in His story of two sons (Matthew 21:28–32) that those who say they will obey, but don't, are worse off than those who say they will not obey, but do. Jesus echoes this warning in the closing portion of His great Sermon on the Mount:

> *Not everyone who says to me, "Lord, Lord,"*
> *will enter the Kingdom of heaven,*
> *but only he who **does the will of my father** who is in heaven.*
> (Matthew 7: 21. Emphasis added.)

But dying is often hard. A friend in the terminal stages of cancer, put our plight in simple terms, when he exclaimed to me, "I don't mind dying. It's getting there I don't like!"

In an effort to provide relief during these end times, society, in recent years, has begun to ease restrictions on terminating life for the old and infirm. It's been a slippery slope!

- At first, we prolonged life using every resource.
- Next, we allowed death to happen naturally.
- Then some said it seemed only right for individuals to decide for themselves when and how to die.
- Later, some physicians, despite the oft quoted pledge to do no harm, began to assist in patient suicides.
- The obvious final step is to have the government or others make the decision when it is time for older people under their control not simply to be allowed to die naturally, but actually be assisted into the chamber of death.

As I once heard a speaker describe the gradual path downward:

> "The unthinkable becomes thinkable;
> the thinkable becomes doable;
> the doable becomes the norm."

So where do we draw the line?

It is best, of course, when we can make such decisions ourselves. Since I am in my eighties and a follower of Jesus and believe in a Biblical world view, I looked primarily at Scriptures to finalize my decision. Set forth below are five Bible passages and five Biblical character sketches that were especially helpful for me.

I pray they will aid you, also.

Five Scriptures Showing God Decides When We Live and Die
(Emphasis added.)

1. God determined the times set for each of us.

*From one man he made every nation of men, that they should inhabit the whole earth; and **he determined the times set for them** and the exact places where they should live. (Acts 17:26)*

2. God ordained all our days before we were born.

*My frame was not hidden from you when I was made in the secret place.
When I was woven together in the depths of the earth,
your eyes saw my unformed body.*

> *All the days ordained for me were*
> *written in your book before one of them came to be.*
> (Psalm 139:15–16)

3. **God has plans for us, and we don't know when, where or how He may want to use us.**

> *And who knows but that you have come to royal position*
> ***for such a time as this?***
> (Esther 4:14b)

4. **There is a "beautiful" time to die.**

> *There is a time for everything, and a season*
> *for every activity under heaven:*
> ***a time to be born and a time to die…***
> *He has made everything **beautiful in its time**…*
> (Ecclesiastes 3:1–2a, 11a)

5. **Sometimes I am to wait for the "appointed time."**

> *For the revelation awaits **an appointed time**;*
> *it speaks of the end and will not prove false.*
> *Though it linger, wait for it;*
> *it will certainly come and will not delay.*
> (Habakkuk 2:3)

Five Stories About Bible Characters Who Learned It Is up to God When, Where and How We Are to Die.

1. Job—refused to "Curse God and die," but received relief only when he surrendered and let God have His way.

The story of Job poses the ancient and timeless question:

"Why do 'good' people suffer?"

Job is tested by losing his children, his possessions, and his health. In chapter 2:9–10 he is urged to take his life, but he refuses:

His wife said to him, "Are you still holding on to your integrity? Curse God and die!"
He replied, "You are talking like a foolish woman. Shall we accept good from God, and not trouble?"

Job "cursed the day of his birth" (Job 3:1) but refused to give up his faith in God, saying,

Though he slay me, yet will I hope in him… (Job 13:15a)

At the end of the story, Job finally surrenders—not because he understands, but because he finally sees who he is compared to

God. When that happens he stops fighting against God's plan for his life, submits to God's will, and concludes:

> *Then Job replied to the Lord: "I know that you can do all things;*
> ***no plan of yours can be thwarted.** You asked,*
> *'Who is this that obscures my counsel without knowledge?'*
> *Surely I spoke of **things I did not understand,***
> ***things too wonderful for me to know...***
> *My ears had heard of you but now my eyes have seen you.*
> *Therefore, I despise myself and repent in dust and ashes."*
> (Job 42: 1–3, 5–6. Emphasis added.)

My Lesson from Job

Job's life became good again, *after he submitted* to God:

> *The Lord blessed the latter part of Job's life*
> *more than the first...*
> (Job 42:12a)

> *After this, Job lived a hundred and forty years;*
> *he saw his children and their children to the fourth generation.*
> *And so he died, old and full of years.*
> (Job 42:16–17)

How sad it would have been for Job, his posterity and countless others, including ourselves, who have been encouraged by Job's struggle and ultimate victory, if he had followed his wife's suggestion to "Curse God and die!"

2. Moses—wanted to live to cross over into the Promised Land but was told to go up on Mount Nebo and die.

After forty years with Pharaoh, followed by forty years of exile in the desert, and forty years of leading the Hebrews out of Egypt and wandering with them in the Sinai wilderness, Moses understandably wanted to complete the journey into the Promised Land. His desire was obvious as he recounts in Deuteronomy 3:23–25:

> *At that time I pleaded with the Lord: "O Sovereign Lord,*
> *you have begun to show to your servant your greatness*
> *and your strong hand.*
> *For what god is there in heaven or on earth*
> *who can do the deeds and mighty works you do?*
> *Let me go over and see the good land beyond the Jordan—*
> *that fine hill country and Lebanon."*

Instead, God commanded him:

> *Go up…to Mount Nebo in Moab, across from Jericho,*
> *and view Canaan, the land I am giving the Israelites*
> *as their own possession.*
> *There on the mountain that you have climbed you will die…*
> (Deuteronomy 32:49–50a)

> *Then Moses climbed Mount Nebo from*
> *the plains of Moab to the top of Pisgah,*
> *across from Jericho. There the Lord showed him the whole land…*
> *Then the Lord said to him, "This is the land I promised on oath*
> *to Abraham, Isaac and Jacob when I said, 'I will give it to your descendants.'*
> *I have let you see it with your eyes, but you will not cross over into it."*

And Moses the servant of the Lord died there in Moab,
as the Lord had said...
Moses was a hundred and twenty years old when he died,
yet his eyes were not weak nor his strength gone.
(Deuteronomy 34:1–7)

My Lesson from Moses

Moses was alert and strong, not dying because he wanted to, but because God commanded it. I have wondered how Moses died. Was it a weak heart in a strong body stressed from climbing the mountain? Perhaps a lightning bolt in a mountain storm? I decided it was immaterial. The lesson was about obedience—not timing or cause of death.

Who knows what tragedies would have befallen Moses and those who followed him, had he disobeyed God and crossed into the land he was forbidden to enter. And how disappointing and destructive to our faith it would have been for us to read of Moses's great miracles in Egypt followed by parting the Red Sea and receiving the Ten Commandments only to see him fall and fail at the end of his life!

3. Elijah—wanted to die but was told to get up and live.

After a great victory over the prophets of Baal at Carmel, Elijah ran for his life down to Beersheba, where he spoke with God as related in 1 Kings 19:3–21,

He came to a broom tree, sat down under it
and prayed that he might die.

> *"I have had enough, Lord," he said, **"Take my life;**
> *I am no better than my ancestors.* (Emphasis added.)

God provided an angel who fed Elijah. He then traveled to Mount Horeb and went into a cave. Again God accosted him and said, "What are you doing here, Elijah?"

He replied that he was the only one of God's prophets who was left. God then told him to "stand on the mountain in the presence of the Lord." Elijah obeyed, and experienced "wind," "earthquake," "fire," and finally a "gentle whisper" as God told him where to go and what to do. His life was not over. God used him to perform great and mighty acts, including anointing Elisha to succeed him as prophet. Elijah never died in the traditional sense and was taken to heaven in a whirlwind—and he apparently knew it was going to happen (2 Kings 2:10–11). Later, he appeared with Moses and Jesus on the Mount of Transfiguration (Matthew 17:1–8).

My Lesson from Elijah

If Elijah had decided when he was to die, there would have been no Elisha succeeding him as prophet and pointing others to God; no evidence of God's hand in history by Elijah being taken to heaven in a whirlwind; and probably no presence of Elijah on the Mount of Transfiguration with Moses and Jesus. How much poorer the world, Elijah, Elisha, and you and I would be if Elijah had decided when he was to die.

4. **Jesus—asked God to "take this cup from me," but acknowledged God's will over His own desires.**

Jesus was the supreme example of following God's will and not our own will when death is near. Kneeling to pray in the Garden of Gethsemane before His crucifixion, Jesus poured out His desire to avoid further pain and agony:

> *Jesus went out as usual to the Mount of Olives,*
> *and his disciples followed him.*
> *On reaching the place, he said to them, "Pray that you will not fall into*
> *temptation." He withdrew about a stone's*
> *throw beyond them, knelt down and prayed,*
> *"Father, if you are willing, take this cup from me;*
> ***yet not my will, but yours be done."***
> *An angel from heaven appeared to him and strengthened him.*
> *And being in anguish, he prayed more earnestly,*
> *and his sweat was like drops of blood falling to the ground.*
> (Luke 22:39–44. Emphasis added.)

How comforting it is to know that the Lord of the Universe had the same temptation we do: namely, to live or die according to *our* will of what will best suit *us*—but that He, in the end, made the decision we are all called to make: namely, that we must live or die according to *God's will* of what will best suit *Him*.

My Lesson from Jesus

No man in history has affected mankind as much as Jesus. It is unimaginable what life would have been like for us all if there had been no sacrifice for our sins; no redeemer to pay our debt back to God; no forgiveness of sin; no salvation of the world; no hope for a wayward humanity including you and me. Oh, God!—Thank you that Jesus showed us the way for us all to finish our lives as he uttered the phrase that has resounded down through the succeeding centuries:

> "...yet not my will, but yours be done"

5. **Paul—wanted to go and be with the Lord but remained because of the needs of others, until God called him home at a later date.**

The Apostle Paul lived a life of incredible danger and hardship. He describes some of his encounters in 2 Corinthians 11:23b–28:

> *I have worked much harder, been in prison more frequently, been flogged more severely, and been exposed to death again and again. Five times I received from the Jews the forty lashes minus one. Three times I was beaten with rods, once I was stoned, three times I was shipwrecked, I spent a night and a day in the open sea, I have been constantly on the move. I have been in danger from rivers, in danger from bandits, in danger from my own countrymen, in danger from Gentiles; in danger in the city, in danger in the country, in danger at sea; and in danger from false brothers. I have labored and toiled and have often gone without sleep; I have known hunger and thirst and have often gone without food; I have been cold and naked. Besides everything else, I face daily the pressure of my concern for all the churches.*

But when we read of Paul's protection from the series of near-death experiences, recorded in Acts 20 to 28 summarized below, it becomes clear that God has overarching care and control of His servants until their work is finished:

1. Paul is "compelled by the Spirit" to go to Jerusalem for the purpose of "testifying to the gospel of God's grace" even though he is warned "that prison and hardships are facing me" (Acts 20:22–24).

2. Paul does testify to the Jews at the Jerusalem temple, resulting in an angry Jewish mob "trying to kill him…." He is saved by Roman soldiers (Acts 21:31–32).

3. Later, as Paul testifies to the Jewish Sanhedrin,

> *The dispute became so violent that the commander was afraid Paul would be torn to pieces by them. He ordered the troops to go down and take him away from them by force and bring him into the barracks.*
> (Acts 23:10)

4. *The following night the Lord stood near Paul and said,*

> *"Take courage! As you have testified about me in Jerusalem, so you must also testify in Rome."*
> (Acts 23:11)

5. The Romans move Paul to Caesarea the next night when they are alerted that

> *more than forty of them (Jews) are waiting in ambush for him.*
> *They have taken an oath not to eat or drink until they have killed him.*
> (Acts 23:12–35)

6. For over two years Paul is held in prison and has the opportunity to testify to his captors (Acts 24–26).

7. After appealing to Caesar, Paul sails for Rome. During a violent storm Paul tells his captors,

> *But now I urge you to keep up your courage,*
> *because not one of you will be lost;*
> *only the ship will be destroyed.*
> *Last night an angel of the God whose I am and whom I serve*
> *stood beside me and said, "Do not be afraid, Paul.*
> *You must stand trial before Caesar;*
> *and God has graciously given you the lives of all who sail with you."*
> (Acts 27:22–24)

8. The Roman soldiers on the ship save Paul from being killed by sailors after it is shipwrecked on Malta (Acts 27, especially verses 42–43).

9. On Malta, Paul is bitten by a viper but suffers no ill effects (Acts 28:3-6).

10. After all these harrowing experiences, Paul arrives safely in Rome and for two years he completes the assignment as he

> *…boldly and without hindrance preached the kingdom of God*
> *and taught about the Lord Jesus Christ.*
> (Acts 28:17–31)

Throughout all these experiences, God protected Paul from death, time after time, until his work was through and he "finished the race," as described so eloquently in his second letter to Timothy. But it obviously was a life of suffering and Paul was human enough to long for the peace, quiet, and security of going home to heaven. As Paul languishes in prison, he writes to believers in Philippi (Philippians 1:20–26) and tells them of the inner struggle he faces—and the decision he makes, and why:

I eagerly expect and hope that I will in no way be ashamed,
but will have sufficient courage so that now as always Christ will be
exalted in my body, whether by life or by death.
For to me, to live is Christ and to die is gain.
If I am to go on living in the body, this will mean fruitful labor for me.

Yet what shall I choose? I do not know! I am torn between the two:
I desire to depart and be with Christ, which is better by far;
but it is more necessary for you that I remain in the body.
Convinced of this, I know that
I will remain, and I will continue with all of you
for your progress and joy in the faith,
so that through my being with you again
your joy in Christ Jesus will overflow on account to me.

In essence, Paul made the decision Jesus mandates for all of us if we are to follow him: to die to our own desires and give up our lives daily, for the benefit of others, until He calls us home.

When God decides our journey is over, there is a "beautiful" time to die, not because we want it, but because God determines it! Ultimately, Paul did know when his "time" finally arrived, and he was being called to go home. He describes it this way in 2 Timothy 4:6–8:

> *For I am already being poured out like a drink offering,*
> *and the time has come for my departure. I have fought the good fight,*
> *I have finished the race, I have kept the faith.*
> *Now there is in store for me*
> *the crown of righteousness, which the Lord,*
> *the righteous Judge, will award to me*
> *on that day—and not only to me, but also to*
> *all who have longed for his appearing.*

My Lesson from Paul

Paul profited from his obedience. But so have countless others. It is difficult to imagine the number of people who have read these passages and then moved on through life to complete whatever God has foreordained for them. How poor we would all be if we had not heard these stirring words and witnessed what it means to "finish the race" and receive the "crown." It is frightening to think what would have happened if Paul had stained his model as a disciple by yielding to his desire and departing before *God* determined it was time!

Conclusion

In the final analysis it becomes clear that the real issue is not one of timing—but of obedience. God calls some of us to come to Him when we would prefer to stay here awhile longer; and he tells some of us to stay here, when we would rather come home to Him. But it is God's decision and not ours to make.

I suppose many of us resonate with David when he asked God:

> *Show me, Oh Lord, my life's end and the number of my days…*
> (Psalm 39:4a).

But like Scrooge in the Dickens' tale, it might frighten us beyond measure if God complied. Therefore, we are probably much more comfortable simply trusting Him with the issue of how and when we shall end life, just as we have trusted Him for so many years to lead us in the life He has given us to live. And surely that must include the end of life decisions we will need to make as we prepare to go home to Him.

Sometime ago a man challenged me by saying, "I sure hope you don't mess up in these later years, because I am watching you!"

Whether we like it or not, someone is watching *each* of us. We don't want to deny God in our final days, and neither do we want to lead others astray who may be following us. I think most of us desire to give God our best—and also give those who are left behind the best example we can of what it means to live, and to finish, a Godly life. Perhaps we can be like an older saint approaching life's end who was told by his Pastor, "You taught me how to live," answered simply, "Now I am going to teach you how to die!"

The Bible indicates that means letting God decide when, where, and how we shall die, just as He decided when, where, and how we are born. He has loved us from the beginning, and we can trust Him to continue to love and care for us until He calls us home.

We sometimes speak of heroes of the faith. For me, the long-suffering ones who endure to the end are such heroes! Unsung, sometimes alone or even forgotten, often in pain and living out the balance of their lives dependent upon God and others for their most basic needs, and doing it with a grace and beauty that brings tears to our eyes and courage to our hearts. They are living ambassadors of the humble Christ who calls to us, "Follow Me!"

I want always to be grateful and give thanks that they faithfully finished their race! In the meantime, I pray God will give us all the strength, faith, fortitude, and patience we need to follow their example and let Him be in control—until we meet in Heaven.

At our age, that may not be too long!

From Grandpa With Love

Part V
Saying Goodbye!

For I am already being poured out like a drink offering,
and the time has come for my departure.
I have fought the good fight,
I have finished the race, I have kept the faith.
(2 Timothy 4: 6–7)

Preface

November, 2009

During the winter and spring of 2009, I felt strongly the need to write what is now contained in Part IV "Who Determines the Time to Leave?" Since we are in our eighties, I mentioned more than once to my wife Ellie that I wondered if God was calling me home soon, since He so impressed me with the need to get the writing completed.

As the days went by, I continued trying to finish and send what had been written to our family and friends, but I could never get what the Bible calls "the peace of God" (Philippians 4:6–7). And so I waited.

What neither of us comprehended was that it was Ellie, not me, who God was getting ready to call home. She left us on September 2, 2009.

After Ellie was gone, it became clear the study had initially been given to prepare us for the difficult experience that was soon to take place, and He was pressing me to complete it before that happened.

I am so glad I waited. The study gave much peace and comfort as we walked through our last chapter and thought of God's hand directing the lives of others who have gone before us—and I knew in my heart that He would lead us in the same way. As you will see from the following pages, He did.

Marriage

In essence, Part IV "Who Determines the Time to Leave?" gives some Biblical principles and a series of sketches about the end of life decisions made by five Biblical characters. By contrast, Part V "Saying Goodbye" relates our own personal experience as a loved one accepts God's control of the time of her departure.

Part IV discusses what happened to others, thousands of years ago. Part V happened to us, now. Each part was necessary to understand the whole. Both have been invaluable.

The story I am going to relate is really Ellie's story, but because God made us "one" when we were married sixty-one years ago, it seems partially mine, too. It also involves our family and all the others who have loved us and helped us during these difficult days.

In any event, I believe Ellie would agree that the rest of the story—about how life ended for her—should be told, so that others we love can be encouraged to look ahead and make Godly decisions as they approach the end of life.

Remember, we all err, so test what I say, hold onto what is good (of God)—and discard the rest.

This is just one person's story, but I hope it is helpful.

From Grandpa With Love

Saying Goodbye!

I suppose the end of life really begins for all of us the day we are born, since we are all mortal. Thus, all the decisions we make along the way, about how we live, what risks we take, etc., have ramifications for how and when we will end our journey. But in the next few pages, we will concentrate on the last few years of Ellie's life, with special emphasis on her final days when the "time came for (her) departure" and she "finished the race." This is the pattern used in the Gospel accounts to help us think about the life, death, and resurrection of our Lord Jesus, and it seems a good model for us to follow as we think on the conclusion of Ellie's life—and also our own lives.

The Question

As we age, many of us find ourselves increasingly asking:

> "How can *we* know when *we* reach the "beautiful" time to die?" (Ecclesiastes 3:1–2a, 11a).

> "How can *we* know when we come to the time God has "determined" for *us*?" (Acts 17:26).

> "How can *we* know, like Paul, that one time it is too early for us to die, and yet be aware at a later time, that the time has come for *our* departure"? (Philippians 1:20–26; 2 Timothy 4:6–8).

Marriage

As Ellie and I walked through these years, it gradually became apparent that we *didn't know* when it *wasn't* the time—but we *did know* when it *was* the time. Let me explain.

We Didn't Know When It Wasn't Time
When we look back at our lives, many of us have a series of incidents, any of which might have proved to be "our time." Ellie was no exception. Over the years, she had many serious medical events, including the births of our five children and several operations. Each time she was blessed by the help received from medical advances and the medical community who treated her and helped her as she moved through those difficult times.

Her most serious event occurred in 1991. During the late summer or early fall of that year, Ellie told me she had experienced a strange event in which she felt almost as if she were about to pass out, while she was working in her flower garden. Despite my urging, she declined to discuss it with her doctor. On November 24, 1991, Ellie reached her sixty-fifth birthday. I felt strongly the uneasy responsibility to prepare a small plaque to present to her, with wording that read eerily like an epitaph. A few days later, while she was having her regular physical exam, Ellie mentioned the garden episode to her doctor. He scheduled a heart catheter procedure, after which he told us she had a severe blockage in a major artery. She underwent successful bypass surgery the next day, December 18, and returned home on Christmas Day 1991.

It seemed such a close call, and yet it was not the end. The operation probably extended her life, until she left us on September

2, 2009. She blessed us greatly all during those extra seventeen years, for which we will be forever grateful.

We Did Know When It Was Time
Although we couldn't know at the time whether Ellie would live through each of the events mentioned above, it is clear in retrospect that none of the incidents were Ellie's "time."

But this all changed beginning about eight years ago, when she began the last chapter of her journey. It became apparent to both of us during the years that followed that God was now calling her home. The illness that was plaguing her would probably be fatal, and she had begun what some have named, "The Long Goodbye." While not as dramatic, it seemed a bit like Paul's journey we discussed earlier in Part IV "Who Determines The Time To Leave?" as he was called to testify in Jerusalem and then in Rome and his life was spared over and over again until he completed his assignment years later.

Ellie's growing awareness that her life was slowly moving to an end was summarized in the following comments we prepared for the booklet given to those who attended her Memorial Service on September 8, 2009.

Walking Home With Jesus
Early in 2001 Ellie became aware that she was suffering memory loss. As the years have gone by and Ellie's health declined, her faith grew ever stronger. Beginning in 2001 she had a series of dreams that made it clear that she was soon going home to Heaven. We thought it might be helpful to you to see a few journal entries made along the way.

Marriage

7-30-01   *Ellie tells me of her dream about a "light" followed by your word to her to "Be Ready." Thanks that she felt a "peace" about it as I do. But help us to "Be Ready."*

12-7-03   *Ellie tells me that a few days ago she either dreamed or had a vision that she walked along and realized she was walking with Jesus—hand in hand! It was almost as if she were watching from above. As she deals with memory loss, she says she knows He will walk with her. This, with her earlier view of the light and the words, "Get Ready!" make her believe God is preparing her.*

11-16-04   *Ellie has another "dream" from God yesterday. As she lay on her bed she saw all the family surrounding her "death bed." She looked up and was so pleased. She said, "Do you know what I am most pleased about? You all know Jesus!" What a wonderful gift You have given her.*

1-24-05   *Ellie continues to feel something is happening to her. Yesterday, she said she "did not feel she would be here long." She says she "feels something is going on inside her." Whatever is happening, we both **trust You completely, Father.**"*

2-28-05   *Ellie is having some more evidence of aging. But two or three days ago she said, "I do not know what is happening, but this is a wonderful time of life!" We laugh and cry—but always with a **very deep** sense, "That all is well!"*

5-29-07   *Ellie dreamed last night she had a heart attack, and a few days ago I dreamed I was preparing a memorial for her. It seems death is much on our minds and in our lives. Help us to walk this last part of life with You.*

During the last two years her condition has steadily declined. The final stage set in about the middle of August, 2009, when she took a dramatic turn and started to experience a series of painful physical symptoms in various parts of her body. By Saturday, August 22, she had developed such throat pain and difficulty in swallowing that she was unable to eat or drink. After various inconclusive tests at the hospital, she returned home on Wednesday, August 26. Since then her family has surrounded her with love and care until her death.

Now her "Walk" is over and she is "Home!"

The Last Four Years—2005 to 2009
In the summer of 2005, Ellie calmly announced to me as we stood together in the utility room of our home, "It's time to go to Larksfield!"(a senior retirement center) So we did.

After we had been in our new apartment for a while, she mused quietly one day, "I get it. You come here to die!"

Interestingly, her conclusion was later echoed by another older resident who lamented, "I think this is God's 'waiting room!'"

As it became more and more clear to Ellie that she could not get well, she embraced rather than fought the conclusion. In the spring of 2008 she commented to me that she wanted to hear the Prayer Breakfast talk (where I was to speak) and then she was ready to go. She continued to voice the same sentiment over the following months.

She never feared or dreaded her pending move to Heaven. We had each drawn living wills to make our wishes known about limiting treatment for terminal illnesses. She signed a "DNR" (Do Not Resuscitate) order. She used medicines to alleviate pain, slow her memory loss, and improve her general health, and well-being. But after a rather stressful "stress test" to check the condition of her heart, she exclaimed, "What am I doing?" That was the end of heart checkups. And her heart condition never contributed to her death. Instead, God had other plans for her.

After Ellie became aware that God was calling her home, she never tried to speed up the time she was to leave and neither did she try to slow it down. And as you will see later, she did not want others to slow down her trip, either. Perhaps it is like any other call of God. Once it comes, we shouldn't hesitate or try to interfere—just obey.

We talked openly between ourselves and also with our family about the naturalness of death. Reality is not pessimism. It is truth. She was comfortable with both.

Ellie was my hero! Once she said, "The one thing I didn't want to lose was my mind." It was as if God was taking the one most precious element of her person. And He was. He cautioned in Luke 14:33,

> *In the same way, any of you who does not give up everything he has cannot be my disciple.*

Gradually, and relentlessly, she did just that as she increasingly gave up memory and accepted the physical limitations that followed. She never complained. She never was angry at God. She was only continually grateful for all she had received and was still receiving in life. And she never lost her sense of humor.

Some have asked, "Did Ellie suffer?" If the reference was to physical pain, that only occurred during the last few days. But once you realize that a person knows they are losing their mental and physical abilities, and that finally they will be totally unable to function, then my answer is, "Yes, she suffered—greatly."

If you can't drive a car, or cook a meal, or read a book, or turn on a television set or radio, or make a phone call, or write a letter, I think you suffer. And if you can't go into a bathroom alone because you can't find how to get out, I also think you suffer. Years ago some friends and I went on a fishing trip up into the wilderness area of Wyoming. One of us became separated from the rest. When we chided him after we found him, he didn't find any humor and said soberly, "You've never been lost or you wouldn't laugh."

How I felt for Ellie and each person in similar circumstances when I thought of the disoriented sensation they must experience feeling lost! If you totally rely on others to keep you safe, it must be like being in a foreign country entirely dependent on your guide. How thankful I am that God allowed people she loved to be there for her.

The key seemed to be the assurance that she was loved, even when she didn't feel useful in the eyes of the world. Ellie *was* loved, and she *knew* it. It seemed a day did not go by without the words, "I love you!" Age and limitations often increase our tenderness and our willingness to give and receive God's love. One of our grandchildren remarked, "Your apartment is like a honeymoon spot." Sometimes, it felt that way to us. In some ways, the last few years were much like the open love and affection most of us feel and express so intensely in our early years of marriage. How we enjoyed the words and notes we exchanged. And words and acts of love came constantly from her family and friends.

During the last years, children and grandchildren who lived close by, came several hours a week to show their love by being with her. Those who lived farther away expressed it by their calls, letters, and visits. It was obvious that times with family and friends were the highlight of her life.

Ellie was a server and she wanted to express her love by helping others. Tearfully, she would say she couldn't do anything, and then with heartfelt gratitude she would thank God and others for what they did for her, and that continued to the end. She was always the most gracious receiver I ever met. In early years, it was for occasional gifts or service; at the end, it was for every small detail of life.

The further we walked into the journey, the more grateful and loving Ellie became. She was always the most other-oriented person I have ever known. As the disease progressed, she became even more so. Tasks became more and more difficult for her—and less and less important to her. Jesus and people were her anchors. She could take forever to get down the hall of our retirement center as she spoke to person after person, holding their hand, or kissing their cheek, and always absorbed in their lives, not her own.

Ellie really enjoyed Larksfield. She never tired of looking out our third floor window at the beauty of a sunrise or sunset as it spread across the sky and its rays flashed like fire from the cross atop the church we could see in the distance. Or watching a full moon and the city lights in the distance. Often she would call me to share the moments with her.

Gradually, we were able to laugh at our own foibles. In December of 2008, Ellie put liquid soap, rather than dry dishwasher soap, in the automatic dishwasher. A short time later she came in and said, "I think you better come into the kitchen." When we arrived, the dishwasher was going strong—soap suds were escaping from every crevice, and pouring into the room—and it looked exactly like an old time movie! We spent part of the rest of the evening scooping soap suds from the dishwasher and floor and trying to get them down the drain. And then laughing together till we cried!

Music and old movies became increasingly important. In the evenings when we finished dinner and started a show, if I came to sit beside her she would smile and ask delightedly, "Oh, are you going to sit with me?" We would hold hands, sometimes embrace, and enjoy the hours together. I truly believe these last years were some of the best years of our lives!

Ellie enjoyed many things in life, but it was always people that were the most important! One of the greatest lifetime gifts God graciously gave to Ellie (and also to those of us who were privileged to be with her) was her great love and interaction with people. How kind of God that it never left her, even as she walked through the final period of her life.

The Last Month
Ellie had several opportunities to spend time with family and friends during her last summer. Soon it was August. The month began benignly. In retrospect, I guess the first two weeks were somewhat like the beauty of a sunset just before the sun sinks out of sight. Or the last warm Autumn days of Indian Summer, before the earth shuts down for Winter. Without our being aware of it, God was orchestrating the first half of the month so that Ellie could have final celebrations with her family and friends, before she started for Home.

August 1–August 12
On Saturday, August 1, we gathered around the table with some of our lifelong friends for a reunion of our Supper Club. At the close of our time together, I mentioned to Ellie, "If we have a reunion next year, I don't think we will all be here." Little did we realize that within a few weeks, both Ellie and another dear friend in the group would be gone. We do need to cherish every day.

Sensing that time was slipping away for Ellie, some of our out-of-state families made the decision to come to Wichita during the week of Monday, August 3. It was a special time for her, with one-on-one visits with children and grandchildren and a luncheon with our three daughters as they shared a "Girl's Day" together.

On August 5, we had our semiannual physicals, and she also met with her neurologist for her six-month checkup. She passed both with flying colors. In fact, the neurologist suggested there was no need to return unless a problem arose. We are deeply grateful for all the care and concern given to us by our physicians and medical staff over the years. But we were soon to find out that no matter what medical tests show, God will still *determine the time!*

As we started to leave for home, Ellie mused with her typical wry humor, "I am in great shape. No high blood pressure, no heart problem—and no mind!"

On Saturday, August 8, our family gathered to celebrate the joint birthday shared by a four-year-old great grandson and myself. We talked and sang and prayed and just had fun together. It was apparent that Ellie was failing, but none of us realized that the end would come so soon.

During these days she enjoyed going to our Encouragers Sunday School Class she liked so much and having lunch with a couple with whom we shared joint birthdays.

As we look back now, it seems obvious that God was giving her a final opportunity to spend these last few days, doing what she did the best and enjoyed the most—loving and being loved by some of those who were closest to her heart. How gracious He was!

August 13–August 26
Around the middle of August, everything changed dramatically. Without our knowing it, the next few days were going to be some of the most significant and meaningful hours of our lives.

First, came a week of extremely painful myoclonic jerks in Ellie's arms, legs, and back. On Saturday, August 22, she began having difficulty swallowing. On Monday, August 24, she was admitted to the hospital for rehydration and throat tests, which proved to be inconclusive. She was dismissed from the hospital and her records transferred to Hospice on Wednesday, August 26.

It has been said,

> "In the 1800s people spoke openly about death,
> but never about sex.
> Today, we speak openly about sex,
> but never about death."

What a loss and tragedy for both!

Death is as natural as birth. Ecclesiastes 3 tells us both are "beautiful" in their "time." I believe we rob ourselves and future generations if we do not, or will not, participate in this great moment of transition from the visible Kingdom of the World to the invisible Kingdom of God.

I believe these final days changed us as individuals and as a family. By being with our loved one as she finished her race, we deepened our relationship with each other and with God. I would not trade those days and hours and moments for anything in the world. She truly taught us how to die. And much of the fear and concern about death was replaced by love and trust in a loving God and a loving family. Some of the younger children seemed to grow up, and some of us older adults seemed to become more like the "little children" spoken of by Jesus in Matthew 18:3.

Looking back, the events unfold like a slow-motion movie. Sometimes the action stops and hangs in space for a while—then moves on. Sometimes it is hazy and jumbled. Sometimes it makes such a sharp and indelible impression that we know we have been privileged to be very close to eternity. Sometimes we weep. Sometimes we chuckle. And, sometimes, there is such an awareness of the presence of God, that we want to fall on our knees and simply cry out, "Oh, Lord!"

Ellie's faith was so strong that she gave us stability and strength. She was so sure, so confident, so pleased with where she was going, that it was contagious. It was almost as if she dumped all her faith on us as she left.

At one point, as Ellie told me that she felt this was her time, I answered,

> "You aren't mad at anyone; no one
> is mad at you; you are at peace with God;
> and you have done what you came to do."

I can think of no better way to finish her race!

Ellie's humor was contagious. She confided to one of the grandchildren, who was visiting with her at the hospital where they were attempting to find why she couldn't swallow, "When you come to the hospital, don't tell them there is anything wrong, or they will try and fix it!" When the attendant noted that her blood type was A+, she quipped, "That's the only A+ I ever received." And later, she said almost to herself, "I hope mucous is worth something, because I sure have a lot of it."

Ellie seemed to know, like Moses, Elijah, and Paul, that this was her time, and she made it clear she did not want anyone interfering with her trip. As we stopped at the elevator going to a test for her throat problem, she announced firmly in her raspy whisper, "I want to say something. I am eighty-two years old. I do not want anything more done to keep me alive!"

She clearly had God's "peace" about finishing her race.

But I learned that it isn't just the patient who needs the "peace of God" in these circumstances. It is also needed by their loved ones. Looking back, I now realize that I had no peace, until we went to the hospital where they could give her rehydration and run throat tests to determine if there was some obvious solution. When there was none, I, too, finally felt His peace.

The Bible says that the "peace of God...transcends all understanding." (Philippians 4:6–7) Since it is beyond understanding, I know of no way to tell someone when they have it. Yet I hear person after person agree that they *do know* when it arrives. And I believe we can know—if we truly seek God's will and are willing to follow it.

As I sat by her bedside at the hospital on Wednesday, August 26, waiting for the order transferring her records to hospice, she asked, "Am I going to die?"

"Yes," I answered. "You know we have talked about it."

She then asked, "How long do I have?"

I responded, "Well, you aren't eating or drinking, so it can't be too long. A few days—perhaps a week."

She was quiet for a moment, and then whispered matter-of-factly, "Well, let's get on with it!"

That was Ellie!

Finishing The Race
The hospital stay and rehydration probably cost Ellie a week of additional suffering, but it was also a great gift. It gave all the family time to come home and spend the final week with her and one another before she left us. I believe it was one of the most significant times of our lives.

I explained to our children that I was unable to care for her alone, and that I needed help. Either from them or from nurses we could bring in. They conferred among themselves and announced that they wanted to care for her themselves. Setting up two-person teams with twelve-hour shifts, they took over. I was there loving and being loved, but for the rest of Ellie's life, they took care of her physical needs and medications as prescribed by the professionals. Their loving care, together with our pastor's visits and prayers and the help from hospice, were of enormous comfort. I believe Ellie was deeply grateful, and so was I.

On Friday, August 28, we quietly celebrated our sixty-first wedding anniversary. The event went almost unnoticed as we dealt with these last days. At night and sometimes during the days, I lay quietly beside her with my head or my hand resting on this nineteen-year-old girl who was now suddenly age 82.

Never was she alone. Always someone was there. Some sang. Some talked. Some prayed. Some sat quietly holding her hand. Some stood a few moments by her bedside. Some offered a sip of broth or tea. Some cared for a personal need. We were all simply loving her. And what a joy it was—because she had loved every one of us!

Despite the turmoil, her compassion remained steadfast. She knew she wasn't suffering alone. At one point she reached up and cupped her daughter's face in her hands and whispered, "Don't cry for my pain, Honey. It's part of the process."

At first she continued to be "our Ellie." But as the days and the hours moved by, she gradually began to leave us. Slowly she moved in and out of consciousness. Always gracious. Always giving thanks. Never complaining.

As we aged in recent years, I had occasionally told Ellie that I felt as if I was at the airport, waiting for them to call my flight! Now, as I sat beside her bedside during her final lucid hours, she said wistfully, "I wish we could take the same flight." I responded, "So do I, but I can't come now."

Then I added, "But I hope to catch another flight soon."

As we approached the final days, and she could no longer communicate with us, I remember telling her as I sat by her bed,

"I feel as if you have taken off and that you are already in the air heading for Heaven, and I am waving 'Goodbye' to you as you go."

The end came very peacefully for Ellie. The hospice people had told us to watch for a change in breathing as one of the signs that her departure time was growing near. At about 8:00 p.m. on Wednesday, September 2, one of our grandchildren, who was sitting next to her bed, called into the living room and said, "I think you better come in. Grandma's breathing is changing."

I sat down beside her, held her hand and we all watched and talked softly as she labored and her breathing became more and more irregular. Then it stopped. After a few moments she gave one giant sigh and left us.

Her "departure time" was 8:20 p.m. Wednesday, September 2, 2009.

Life Still Goes On
Ellie's middle name was Ruth. She was at our daughter's bedside when she gave birth to a little girl who was given the middle name of Ruth, in honor of Ellie. It was this granddaughter, now grown up and married, who had called us to come into the bedroom a few moments before. In the stillness after Ellie's final breath, she said quietly, "Grandma was with me when I was born. I am with Grandma when she died."

Life is a continuum. It doesn't begin when we are born and it will not end when we die. God is doing something in history, and He has allowed us to be in on it. How grateful I am that He gave us Ellie for our time in history, and that He has now taken her back to be with Him. And that we can all join them both later, if we will simply surrender and follow Jesus so we can someday live together in the home He has gone to prepare for us in Heaven.

As Ellie's earthly form lay quietly on the bed, most of the others slowly drifted out of the room. I leaned over and kissed her forehead and her lips, and told her once more how much I loved her. Then it was over, and I, too, left the room.

Ellie is now with the Lord for eternity. I am so pleased for her. And I am so grateful to God for taking her home when she was ready to go and it was clearly the time He had chosen and determined for her. I am also thankful for the family and loved ones who loved and supported us as we told her,

"Goodbye."

A Final Word

I'm not sure who I thought was to read what I have written. I only know I had to write it. I felt like Elihu, who cried out in frustration:

> *For I am full of words and the spirit within me compels me;*
> *inside I am like bottled-up wine, like new wineskins ready to burst...*
> *I must speak and find relief;*
> (Job 32:18–20a)

Perhaps it is because there is such a void after Ellie is gone. She was so much a part of my life and I simply am not whole without her. Perhaps, writing this has been one way of having her with me for a while longer.

In any event, it is done. I have laid down my burden—at least for now.

I suppose the hurt will never be gone, until my journey is over. And that is good, because in that way I know that Ellie is not really gone, and that I will see her again when we all gather together in Heaven.

Until then I close this wonderful chapter of life with these final words:

> **"Thank you, God, for Ellie.**
> **Thank you, Ellie, for everything."**
> Marv

Epilogue

2015

It has now been over five years since Ellie left us in 2009. Since that time much has changed in my life. Much to my surprise, I remarried in 2012, left our retirement center, changed my church home, and began another chapter of life.

Some have asked why I did not include my remarriage in this discussion. One reason is that remarriage at age 86 is so unique that I doubt if there are many others who will ever experience it or profit from my comments.

But more important is the rationale I expressed in the closing "thank you" of *Four Generations*, where I explained:

> While God has graciously given me some additional time and a good remarriage, these additional years seem more of a postscript than a continuation of life as we have known it. We are still connected to our loved ones here. But it is almost as if they were helping us prepare for the ultimate adventure as we move into our space ship with a final crew and get ready to head for Home. There may be a time He wants me to write about this later phase of life, but for now it is time to stop my story.

Again I say, thank you to the Lord and to everyone He has used to teach, help, and contribute to whatever is written here about *Marriage*—one of God's greatest gifts. I appreciate you all!

See You In Heaven!

From Grandpa With Love

Made in the USA
San Bernardino, CA
22 April 2015